PRAISE FOR *EMPOWERING LEADERSHIP*

"Being an Ironman triathlete, Michae[l] is also the key to sustaining healthy s[p] examples from his own experience, compelling insight into Scripture, practical wisdom for leaders at every stage of development, *Empowering Leadership* instructs as well as inspires—highly recommended!"

—Chris Hodges, senior pastor, Church of the Highlands;
author of *Fresh Air* and *The Daniel Dilemma*

"Michael reminds pastors that we need to do more than simply reach the people around us. We need to be raising up other leaders whose influence will go far beyond our own. This book made me excited all over again to help others become leaders who will make an impact beyond anything I could imagine!"

—Greg Surratt, founding pastor, Seacoast Church;
president, Association of Related Churches

"We don't need bigger crowds. We need an army of leaders to change the world. Michael Fletcher's new work explains clearly how Manna Church has developed the culture and systems to not only deploy leaders in their church, but also to be sent as an army to change the world. *Empowering Leadership* is filled not just with principles but very workable practices based on experience."

—Dave Travis, chief executive and chief
encouragement officer, Leadership Network

"We have all read books on leadership written by people who have not done what they urge others to do. Michael Fletcher is different. He has actually built the leadership culture he describes in this essential book. In *Empowering Leadership*, he gives us the hard-won lessons of his leadership life, and with them we can lead as Michael has led and change our generation in the process."

—Stephen Mansfield, PhD, *New York Times* bestselling author

"From church janitor to megachurch pastor, Michael has been God's instrument to raise up countless ministry leaders from the house, for the house, for the world, and for God's kingdom. This book is the story of how that happened and how God could use you in the same way. This could change everything for your church. Everything."

—Shawn Lovejoy, founder and CEO, CourageToLead.
com; author of *Be Mean About the Vision*

"Michael Fletcher is at the top of the list when it comes to reproducing leaders. He's one of the most strategic and focused leadership generators I know. In *Empowering Leadership* he reveals the paradigms and strategies he has used for decades to find, develop, and release leaders worldwide. If you're involved in any aspect of leadership development, this is a book you need to read."

—Larry Osborne, author and pastor, North Coast Church

"As I began to read *Empowering Leadership*, I couldn't put it down. Michael has hit a grand slam home run! This book is thoroughly biblical and extremely practical at the same time. Michael is not a theoretician but a practitioner of church leadership. I have watched the church he leads grow and thrive even in the most difficult arena. You'll be inspired, motivated, and informed about how to go to the next level. Thanks, Michael, for one of the best ministry leadership books in the kingdom."

—Dr. Chris Stephens, Faith Promise Church

"Today we hear so much about the need for a church to have a leadership pipeline but so little about the culture necessary to produce more and better leaders. Michael Fletcher's book will be an instant 'must read' for those who realize that improving their church's leadership development culture is the only way they'll see 'more and better leaders' produced across all their different ministries."

—Brent Dolfo, leadership development
director, Leadership Network

"Michael Fletcher has been doing the stuff called leadership for nearly forty years. There's no one I know who is better at making disciples, building leaders, and planting churches. *Empowering Leadership* is a practical textbook for anyone wanting to learn how to do the stuff that makes a kingdom impact."

—Steve Robinson, Church of the King

"In a world that pursues and celebrates large crowds, this book is a road map that draws us back to what really matters—creating cultures that develop great leaders. Michael is one of the most influential kingdom leaders of our generation, and his voice is much needed right now. His wisdom has transformed the way I think and the way I lead. Every leader needs to read this long-awaited book with their team."

—John Stickl, lead pastor, Valley Creek Church;
author of *Follow the Cloud*

"*Empowering Leadership* is the simple, profound, biblical solution to the nationwide leadership crisis. Michael shares his own journey and draws us into the right, hard work of taking those around us and developing them to their full potential. Otherwise known as discipleship."

—Jerry Daley, veteran church planter

"My first thought after finishing *Empowering Leadership* was, *This is now going to be my #1 recommended book on leader development.* Pastor Michael Fletcher has clearly outlined a practical system for identifying, developing, and multiplying leaders at all levels."

—Linda Stanley, vice president and team leader, Leadership Network

"In *Empowering Leadership* Michael shares the reasons why and how a church can turn laymen into leaders. It is a jam-packed goldmine of advice, tools, and insights that can propel you and your organization forward with fresh motivation and success."

—Lynette Lewis, author of *Climbing the Ladder in Stilettos*;
TEDx speaker, business consultant, pastor's wife

"As my friend, colleague, and coach, with all I have I can attest that Michael Fletcher loves two things: Jesus and His church. The ideas and principles contained in this book are simply the overflow of these loves. These are not merely hopeful ideas created by a theorist. These are principles learned by a leader of leaders over decades of prayer, study, trial, and failure. They are biblical and proven. If you want to see Jesus glorified by the church reaching the lost and raising up influencers in the world, I can testify from personal experience that this book is for you."

—David McQueen, Beltway Church

"I've had the privilege of watching Michael Fletcher build solid leaders for nearly thirty years. The leadership culture he and his team build is easily transferable via the Upward Draft, Shoulder Tapping, and SERVE Model, just to name a few highlights from this book. I'm honored to endorse Michael, his leadership methodology, and *Empowering Leadership*."

—Ron Lewis, international church planter, Every Nation;
senior minister, Every Nation NYC/ New Jersey and
King's Park International Church, Raleigh-Durham

EMPOWERING
LEADERSHIP

EMPOWERING
LEADERSHIP

HOW A LEADERSHIP DEVELOPMENT CULTURE
BUILDS BETTER LEADERS FASTER

MICHAEL FLETCHER

THOMAS NELSON

Since 1798

Published in Nashville, Tennessee, by Thomas Nelson. Thomas Nelson is a registered trademark of HarperCollins Christian Publishing, Inc.

Thomas Nelson titles may be purchased in bulk for educational, business, fundraising, or sales promotional use. For information, please e-mail SpecialMarkets@ ThomasNelson.com.

Unless otherwise noted, Scripture quotations are taken from the Holy Bible, New International Version®, NIV®. Copyright © 1973, 1978, 1984, 2011 by Biblica, Inc.® Used by permission of Zondervan. All rights reserved worldwide. www. Zondervan.com. The "NIV" and "New International Version" are trademarks registered in the United States Patent and Trademark Office by Biblica, Inc.®

Scripture quotations marked AMP are taken from the Amplified Bible, copyright 1954, 1958, 1962, 1964, 1965, 1987 by The Lockman Foundation. Used by permission. (www.Lockman.org)

Scripture quotations marked ESV are from the ESV® Bible (The Holy Bible, English Standard Version®). Copyright © 2001 by Crossway, a publishing ministry of Good News Publishers. Used by permission. All rights reserved.

Scripture quotations marked NASB are from New American Standard Bible®, Copyright © 1960, 1962, 1963, 1968, 1971, 1972, 1973, 1975, 1977, 1995 by The Lockman Foundation. Used by permission. (www.Lockman.org)

ISBN 978-0-7180-9378-5 (eBook)
ISBN 978-0-7180-9376-1 (TP)

Library of Congress Control Number: 2017957638

Printed in the United States of America
18 19 20 21 22 LSC 10 9 8 7 6 5 4 3 2 1

Dedicated to all those pastors and leaders who work hard every day to help people come to the full potential of their calling. You give people courage and hope. You help them believe in a better tomorrow. You build the future of the church. This is the job!

About Leadership ❈ Network

Leadership Network fosters innovation movements that activate the church to greater impact. We help shape the conversations and practices of pacesetter churches in North America and around the world. The Leadership Network mind-set identifies church leaders with forward-thinking ideas—and helps them to catalyze those ideas resulting in movements that shape the church.

Together with HarperCollins Christian Publishing, the biggest name in Christian books, the NEXT imprint of Leadership Network moves ideas to implementation for leaders to take their ideas to form, substance, and reality. Placed in the hands of other church leaders, that reality begins spreading from one leader to the next . . . and to the next . . . and to the next, where that idea begins to flourish into a full-grown movement that creates a real, tangible impact in the world around it.

NEXT: A Leadership Network Resource
committed to helping you grow your next idea.

leadnet.org/NEXT

CONTENTS

INTRODUCTION

WE DO TWO THINGS WELL

I had no idea what I had gotten myself into, but I was so excited at twenty-six years of age, after serving on staff for three years in a variety of roles, to finally be a senior pastor! We had 350 people, and we were going to change the world! But not, I was soon to realize, until God changed me. First, I had to find out what I didn't have. Then I had to find out what I did have.

WHAT I DIDN'T HAVE

Manna Church was planted during the wild and wooly Jesus People movement from a core of people who attended a Bible study at a halfway house for recovering drug addicts and alcoholics. These were the days when some traditional ideas about church were thrown out the window in favor of an allegedly more–New Testament model of church, which, by the way, no one had any real idea how to produce. In those days, you didn't need any real structure, advertising, or even evangelistic strategies. Just start teaching the Bible and people would show up. The church was planted and led by a tremendous Bible teacher and disciple maker who poured his life into the mostly massively broken people who turned out to listen. Thirteen years later, it was my turn to lead.

I inherited some really great leaders, people who had been discipled into health by our founding pastor. These were great people. They had character, passion, strong families, and a deep commitment to the church. They were great leaders, but they weren't my leaders. Their loyalty was primarily toward the man who had led them into health and the style of church that had helped them get there. A stronger leader could have stepped right into this scenario and done just fine. My problem was that I wasn't as strong a leader as I thought I was. On top of that, I had more knowledge than sense, so I tried to change things too fast. I found myself disappointed and frustrated.

Not by design but by nature, Manna Church was a hospital church. We attracted broken—and I mean really broken—people. We worked six days a week, and our counseling load was overwhelming. In those days there was a counseling revolution under way. The prevailing thought was that biblical counseling was the only way to truly help people. So the local church was the center of restoration for broken people. That sounds good, but it essentially meant all other methods and sources of counseling, therapy, and support were off-limits. We were out of our depth and didn't know it. Thus people with severe problems—sexual addictions; physical, emotional, mental, or spiritual abuse; multiple adulteries; mental illness of every sort; pedophilia and other types of unspeakable perversion; and suicidal depression, to name a few maladies—were lining up at our front door for help. I remember crying out to God, asking Him to send some people with some easy problems, like bitterness. "And while You are at it, please, no more flaky people." No kidding, I really prayed that.

Manna Church is in Fayetteville, North Carolina, right next to the largest military base (per population) in the US armed forces. A full 70 percent of the church was or is related in some way to the military. Also, my wife and I grew up in military families, so we should have known better. We grew up moving every two years, but we completely failed to factor that reality—people moving every few years—into how being in a transient population would affect the church. Each year, often around the summer, the US government would transfer people to other bases around the world. In addition, those who had completed their time in service would exit active duty and return home, almost always to some other part of the country. When this happened in my first year as senior pastor, I didn't even notice. We had grown some, so the numerical impact wasn't significant, and I was still too enamored with the reality that I was the senior pastor.

The second summer was different. I woke up one day to find that the nursery coordinator, children's church director, Sunday school coordinator, and some of their key people had received orders and were being transferred. Our whole children's department was headed out the door in a matter of weeks. Two elders were moving to pursue master's degrees (no distance learning in those days), and another was taking a job in a different state. We were overwhelmed, operating a church that was a spiritual hospital, and Uncle Sam was transferring our leaders away without bothering to ask permission!

At the end of two years, it was clear to me what I didn't have. I was losing the leaders whom someone else had built, and I didn't have the right people in the church to replace them. I needed better people, so I began asking God to send them. Instead, God sent a videotape.

WHAT I DID HAVE

People occasionally give pastors some stuff to read and watch. At first, I felt obligated to read and watch it all, but it wasn't long before a stack began to form on my desk. People would say, "Did you read it?" And I'd say, "It's in the stack." This seemed to satisfy most people, but you can't get away with that when an elder gives you something to watch. After being asked seven or eight times if I'd watched it, I decided I'd have to get this videotape out of the way. I went to the conference room and set the TV/VCR combo (it was the 1980s) at one end of the table. I sat at the other end with other work spread out in front of me. The plan was to watch the video while I worked so I could check off the box of obligation.

The tape was a recording of Pastor Tommy Barnett speaking at his now famous pastors school in Phoenix, Arizona. I listened happily until I heard him say, "All you need to reach your city is already in the house!"

I looked up and thought, *Did he really say what I thought I heard him say?* So I rewound the tape and played it again. Sure enough, there it was: "All you need to reach your city is already in the house." I could not believe my ears! I was incredulous! I said out loud, "That's easy for you to say; you have ten thousand people!" and I let the VCR play on. But my mind was stuck, and I couldn't shake it, so I rewound the tape. Barnett said the same thing. This time I argued. I literally shouted at the TV as if Pastor Barnett could answer me: "You shouldn't tell pastors stuff like that! Some of us have a bunch of people on our hands who are a real mess, and it's irresponsible of you to spout trite platitudes like that." I moved on, but I was drawn back to Pastor Barnett's words: "All you need to reach your city is already in the house."

What I didn't realize was that God was speaking to me through Tommy Barnett's words, and there was no escaping that. This time, I stared at the table and asked Barnett, "How in the world can I reach this city with these people—not *these* people." I tried to return to my work, but I couldn't. This time, instead of talking to Tommy Barnett, I talked to God: "Lord, if he is right"—and by this time I knew he was—"then how am I supposed to do this?"

I heard a still, small voice whispering in my heart: *"Michael, you don't see these people as I see these people. Everything you need to reach this city is already in the house."*

It was a true breakthrough moment in my life that changed everything. Right then, I knew I had to do two things.

First, we were sitting on a gold mine in terms of the lives of people who had been helped by God. Their stories, their testimonies could fuel the outreach strategy we so desperately needed. With an attrition rate of up to 20 percent due to military transfers and people returning home after separating from active duty, it was clear, even in those early days, if we didn't develop an intentional outreach strategy, we wouldn't survive.

I immediately began giving salvation altar calls every week and training church members to minister to people's basic spiritual needs. We used Evangelism Explosion as our one intentional outreach strategy, and I supplemented outreach by preaching things like "God wants to take our tragedy, turn it into a triumph, to build a testimony." It wasn't much, but it was a start. God blessed our fledgling efforts by adding people to our church every year.

Second, I knew God had already sent what we needed.

There were leaders in the house; they just had to be identified and equipped.

What I did next was something I would not now recommend. I stood in the pulpit, weeks after listening to Pastor Barnett, and said, "If any of you see anything in me that you would like in your life, meet me this Saturday in room 310." About forty people showed up, which dwindled to about thirty over the next month. Saturday morning was a tough day and time, so I shifted the group of all men to Sunday at 6:00 a.m., reasoning that no one would miss a soccer match or a family breakfast or get called into work at that hour. I ended up with about twenty-five faithful guys, some rotating out while others rotated in. Almost all of them grew to become leaders, elders, pastors, missionaries, church planters, or staff members. I had accidentally created my first leadership-development pipeline! That group ran for about twenty years and produced people who are serving in ministry all over the world.

Often, my pastor friends tell me: "Michael, you're crazy! Sunday is your most important day, and you're giving the best of yourself at six o'clock in the morning to twenty-five guys instead of the crowds who gather to attend services."

And I tell them: "That's the difference between you and me. You are preaching to a crowd, and I am building an army of leaders to change the world."

What I thought I needed was what I already had. Inside

the house were people whom God had already deployed all over the city, people whose lives were in the process of being transformed into trophies of His grace. They just had to be sent. God had embedded people who could be developed into world-changing leaders. They just had to be built.

Today, our evangelistic strategy is much more mature and full-bodied than the one we developed back then. This year, we will make more than 400,000 "gospel touches" in the Cape Fear region. Last year, 1,143 people left us through military transfer or moved back home after they ended their time in service. We had to grow 1,143 people just to stay even. And a good number of those were leaders we'd trained, built inside this house, through our leadership-development pipeline.

So we do two things well: outreach and leadership development. In order to survive, we had to learn how to effectively reach people and how to build better leaders faster. So how do we do it? How does it all work? Outreach is the topic of some other book. How to build better leaders faster is the topic of this one.

1

THE LEADERSHIP CRISIS

It happened again. As I sat at my keyboard to write this chapter, I saw an e-mail from a pastor of a large and fast-growing church I had met while mentoring a group of pastors on leadership development. The contents of the e-mail were familiar: "We need to learn how to create a leadership-development culture in our church. May my team and I travel to your church for one day to learn about this?" Yesterday, I spent considerable time on two phone calls about the same topic: how to build better leaders faster. The first was a conference call with a number of pastors who, at the end of the phone call, requested a two-day meeting for their group. The second was with the facilitator of a group of top churches of a certain denomination. This is routine, and it has absolutely nothing to do with me. (Trust me, I'm not being humble. I wish I were humble.) It has everything to do with what I am calling the *leadership crisis*.

According to a World Economic Forum survey, 86 percent of respondents say there is a leadership crisis in the world today.[1] There simply aren't enough trained leaders to meet the political and economic challenges the world is facing today. In a recent *Forbes* magazine article, leadership author Mike Myatt outlined this leadership crisis and actually called for a new leadership movement to solve the problem.[2] Beyond economics and politics, a simple search of the Internet yields numerous articles predicting a leadership crisis in nursing, public school principals, pharmacy, higher education, and so on. And this leadership crisis is not just a secular problem. Ask any pastor.

We simply have more needs inside and outside the local church than leaders to meet those needs, and everyone feels it. As I travel the world (our network of churches has operations in sixty-three countries), consult with churches here in the United States, and serve as a mentor with Leadership Network, it seems everyone is asking the same question: "How do we train better leaders faster?"

Growth requires that we add new leaders. Continual growth requires a continual supply of leaders. The megachurch and multisite movements have proven this point. Additionally, leaders in smaller churches understand that, to move forward, they have to develop a growing team of leaders. The problem is, very few have a well-thought-out leadership-development pipeline, and even fewer have a true leadership-development culture. To fill the roles of staff, churches simply hire from other churches. Therefore, when it comes to building the leadership potential of the individual members of the church, most churches are too busy scrambling to find volunteers to fill slots to even think about leadership development on this level. The church cannot afford to simply pilfer one another's staffs and ignore the massive leadership potential in the pews. Eventually someone is going to have to train some new leaders!

LEADERSHIP DEVELOPMENT ON TWO LEVELS

The local church must concern itself with training leaders on two levels—staff and members—and the second can feed the first.

Hiring pastors and key staff roles from within is the very best policy. If you use the character, chemistry, and competence metric for hiring staff, it only makes sense to hire almost exclusively from within. Since the person was built inside the house—discipled, mentored, trained, developed—the character of the individual is well known. Further, leaders in the house likely had their hands in the formation of that character, since true leadership development includes the often messy but necessary interaction of life upon life. Leaders trained inside the house grow up breathing the culture of the house. You don't have to send them through a ten-week "learn our DNA" program; they are a product of that culture. They don't just know your vision, they are part of it. They own it.

When leaders are built inside the house, their gifts and callings become apparent, their strengths and weaknesses obvious. You are able to evaluate them by what you have gleaned from personal observation as it relates to their competency, not just what you read in a résumé or discerned from a few interviews. Simply put, you know what you're getting when you hire from within.

One very powerful benefit from hiring almost entirely from within is what we call the *upward draft*. When a church member is in a key leadership role and then brought onto the paid staff, the change creates a vacuum of sorts and pulls other leaders up to fill that former position. This, in turn, creates another vacuum, which pulls up others into higher roles of leadership. In one ministry role after another, this readjustment goes all the way down through the ranks.

A true leadership-development culture feeds off the excitement created by the upward draft. This is especially true when the role being filled is a pastor or director slot. The people in the church are being led by someone they think of as "one of us," and the idea that one day that could be me becomes much more than a dream. Or we could just pilfer staff from some other church and send the message to our members that no one here is good enough to fill these roles.

At the time of this writing, we cut about 120 payroll checks per month, including weekenders (those who only work on the weekends). Of those, 113 were built inside the house. Of the four people on our lead team, three started as janitors—and that includes me. As a result, the vast majority of our staff has been thoroughly cross-trained. One pastor served in housekeeping, led worship, served the youth, and worked as a personal assistant before becoming a pastor. Another worked as a janitor, served in children's ministry, youth ministry, and outreach and evangelism before he joined the staff as an administrator and then as a pastor. And I could go on and on.

In fact, we don't hire for specific professional roles, such as children's pastor or youth pastor. We build and hire pastors and put them in various roles to help further develop them in their calling.

For example, our children's pastor has the strongest pastoral gift on the team and will one day be the senior leader of a local church. But to truly reach his potential, we knew he would have to learn how to build and lead teams. So we put this single man with no kids in the role as children's pastor, because there is no better place to learn to build and lead teams. The people love him, and he has grown tremendously in his leadership in this present role. Before that, he was my personal assistant.

Every one of my personal assistants has gone on to become a pastor. I didn't hire them to be my assistant because they were great personal assistants; in fact, a number of them were terrible. I placed them in that role so I could mentor them and help develop them in their calling. It's all part of the upward draft. It's what happens in a leadership-development culture. And it's not complicated; it's just like raising a bunch of kids. That's why most churches don't do it.

Raising a bunch of kids is messy and time-consuming. I'll admit that's true. It's messy. Building people means you have to deal with their immaturity. You have to settle the squabbles generated by sibling rivalries. You have to fix the messes they make because they don't know they're in over their heads. You have to deal with the teenage "I know everything and can never be told" stage. It's time-consuming. Life-upon-life mentoring takes time. It takes time to let leaders learn through failure. It takes time to wait for their character to catch up to their calling. Honestly, it takes less time to buy one (i.e., hire from without) than it does to build one.

I was invited to a two-day meeting of about thirty pastors hosted by some of America's most famous church leaders. Everyone in the meeting led churches. They were from various backgrounds. They were on the Outreach 100 fastest growing or 100 largest lists (or both). We were invited to learn about leadership from a well-respected pastor from another nation who leads one of the largest church movements in the world.

Toward the end of the second day, during a question-and-answer session, the guest asked permission to be completely honest. "I think one of the major problems among leaders in the US," he said, "is that you pilfer staff members from each other's churches. If I speak at your church or your conference, you can trust that I will never, ever try to hire someone off your staff. We build our own because we want them to have our culture and not yours."

Am I saying that we should never hire from the outside? Of course not. There is a time for a leader to leave a church and move to another. Shifts like that can be a healthy part of one's journey with God. There is also a time to bring some fresh blood into a staff by reaching outside your circle. Fresh perspective is important for the advancement of any organization. But I believe the church is called by God to develop people and by and large build its own staff from the people who are being developed in the house.

Creating an upward draft requires that we build leaders *in the house* as well as build pastors *for the house*. Perhaps the most popular evangelistic tract in the United States was "The Four Spiritual Laws," written by Campus Crusade founder Bill Bright. The first proposition is, "God loves you and has a wonderful plan for your life." No matter what you think of evangelistic tracts in general, or this one in particular, that statement is nonetheless true. God loves His people and created them on purpose for a purpose. Their lives have meaning. There is a God-designed reason for them being on this planet, and the best place to discover that is in church.

People walk into our churches asking these questions. People who have not yet met the Lord and people who have followed Him for years are asking these questions. It is our job as church leaders to help them find the answers. And the answer cannot simply be "volunteer to work in our parking lot."

I have a hard time with the notion that God made a man who, according to Psalm 139, was handcrafted in his mother's womb by God Himself whose purpose in life is to serve in a church parking lot two hours per week. Here is a guy who was born into this life, was cared for and nurtured by his parents, has been shaped by God through life, was trained at a fine university in economics and finance, has risen to become the director of client services for a large and popular personal finance consulting firm, interacts daily with the wealthiest and most influential people in the region where he lives—and his purpose is serving in a church parking lot? Seriously?

Get him out of the parking lot. Get some strong believer into his life. Guide him toward the leadership-development pipeline. Equip this man to see himself as the shepherd sent by God to impact the lives of those he serves on a daily basis!

But the press these days is to find volunteers, not build people. We have to find people to fill the slots to feed the machine called *church*. We don't have time to build people because, again, building people is messy and takes time. The problem is, when we look around the church, we see people who are leaders out there in society but aren't leaders in the church. We need to wake up and realize we need more than volunteers! We need leaders in this house! Where are the leaders?

Frustration builds as we recognize that many of these great people just aren't motivated to take key leadership roles. At the same time, less qualified people are willing but aren't ready to step up. They're underdeveloped in their character or competency. So we create a leadership class, but the people we hope will attend often don't. Then we hear someone talk about a leadership pipeline and think we've found the solution. It's a step in the right direction, but it's not worth very much and won't work as advertised if it isn't built on the foundation of a leadership-development culture.

WE NEED A FARM SYSTEM

The St. Louis Cardinals are considered by many people the best baseball franchise in the game today.[3] I'm not saying they are the best team every year, and I'm not predicting they will win the World Series. But they will be in the running. (They are almost every year.) It's about the franchise, not the team. Let me explain.

Major League Baseball is unlike all other US-based sports in that it includes a farm system—not a system of farms that grow vegetables but a system that is like a farm in that they *grow* players. Kids right out of high school, young men from college, and people from other countries who have aspirations to play Major League Baseball eagerly await the draft every year. Players are evaluated by scouts from the various Major League teams and are selected during the draft to play in the farm system of that particular team. Depending on their skill level, players may be drafted to join that MLB farm team in the Rookie League, A League (called Single A), AA League (Double A), or AAA League (Triple A). Very rarely, an extremely gifted athlete may go straight to the Major League team. Often, the managers and coaches of the farm teams are former Major League players from the same franchise. These heroes of the past serve as mentors to these young players and focus on what baseball calls *player development*. As players develop in their professional and personal lives, they move up the ranks as openings occur. This upward draft and the opportunity to be mentored by former major leaguers creates excitement and hope among the younger players.

It used to be that every MLB team was built this way, players being developed and slowly working their way up the system, some even playing in the Major League. But then came free agency, and the game changed. Players were free to leave their teams and sell themselves on the market as free agents. The teams with the most money could buy the best players and skip the player development process. Every team kept the farm system and paid lip service to it, but the real effort and money was in buying the already developed players from the other teams. At least one team, however, never abandoned its almost total reliance on their farm system: the St. Louis Cardinals. (Ironically, the first free agent was a St. Louis Cardinals player.)

The Cardinals put most of their money and effort into the farm system, slowly developing players and teaching them the Cardinal Way. To put it another way, they instill in them the culture and philosophy of the team. That's why the Cardinals' payroll is often less than half of that of the top spending teams. Spending on what? On buying players!

After a number of years of doing business this way, most teams are migrating back to a reliance on the farm system. They realize that buying expensive, already-built players from other teams does not yield the same results as having a steady stream of qualified players waiting in line to fill a role.

During the 2015 season, the Cardinals took the lead with the best record in baseball on April 29 and did not relinquish it throughout the rest of the regular season. And yet they were racked with injuries to their best players throughout the year.[4] How could they pull off such remarkable results? If you looked at the roster at midseason, it was hard to tell if it was a St. Louis Cardinals roster or a Memphis Redbirds roster (the AAA affiliate farm team). These rookies were ready to play at this level because they had been developed. They had been steeped in the culture and developed in the farm system— put another way, built in the pipeline.

At the trade deadline just before the playoffs, teams lined up in a mad scramble to shore up their rosters by buying players from other teams. Predictably, the Cardinals, stocked with players built in house, sat out of the fire sale and won the division—again.

What is baseball? It's a game. A season runs from April through October, and then it's done. People, however, last forever. God has called us to develop people and help build them into the leaders God called them to be. If we put our focus there, we'll never lack for the supply of leaders we so desperately need, and we'll have the farm system to build the staff we've dreamed of. As it turns out, building people *is* the job, and that's the topic of the next chapter.

BUILDING PEOPLE *IS* THE JOB!

The short statement "All you need to reach your city is already in the house" rocked my world! Like many pastors, I had regular thoughts, prayers, and whining sessions about not having what I needed: more leaders, more money, more people, and more of the *right* people. Yet here was Tommy Barnett (and God through him) telling me just the opposite. I already had all I needed in the people who were *already* in the house. I was seeing it all wrong, because I was seeing people all wrong. God didn't send people to build the church. He sent the church to build people. That's the job, the real job: building people.

AN UNFAIR TRADE

Jesus didn't come to earth, clothe Himself in humanity, walk among us for thirty-three years, die on the cross, and ascend to heaven just to start a new organization or a new religion. He came for people—people ravaged by sin and deceived by darkness, people who were far away from God, people who didn't think the way He thought, whose mind-sets were all wrong, people whose lifestyles were built on bankrupt philosophies. He came to redeem them, by trading places with them—the righteous for the unrighteous, the godly for the ungodly—thus restoring them to God.

In a very real sense, it was the Father who made the trade. He was the one who conceived the plan to send the Son to redeem a people for Himself. It's a verse everyone knows: "For God so loved the world that he gave his one and only Son, that whoever believes in him shall not perish but have eternal life" (John 3:16). The Father traded His Son for people who were diametrically opposed to Him, namely, sinners: "But God demonstrates his own love for us in this: While we were still sinners, Christ died for us" (Rom. 5:8).

It is amazing, crazy, scandalous! A perfect God trading a perfect Son for a people who hate Him, a people continually sinning against Him, a people not even seeking Him! It was an unfair trade: people who deserve punishment receiving a place in heaven (through no effort or merit of their own) and the One who deserves heaven (who by right is already possessing it) giving it all away. There must be some mistake!

But then a God who is perfect never makes mistakes. He knew exactly what He was doing, and in doing it, He established the worth of people and, if you have come into relationship with Him through faith, your worth too. Let that sink in a moment. He traded Jesus for you, but not just you: for all those other people who come to know Him by faith as well. A thing is worth whatever someone will pay for it, and the Father purchased you at the price of His Son. He traded Jesus for you! That's what the word *redeemed* means: to buy back. God established your worth in that He gave His own Son to bring you back into relationship with Him.

The first trick is believing that ourselves. The second and sometimes more difficult trick is believing that about others! And that's where I was stuck. I could get my head around the idea that God loved me, justified me by faith, redeemed me for Himself, and had a special plan for my life. Further, I was clear on His plan for me. I was called to build the church. Or was I? Even if I did see people the way God saw people, I faced a perplexing dilemma. How could I build a great church with imperfect people? The answer was simple and right in front of my face!

AN ALL-ENCOMPASSING PLAN

The church was another crazy idea of God's! How in the world could we take people from all walks of life (all of whom are sinners), from greatly varying backgrounds, holding sometimes opposing points of view, at differing levels of sanctification, and pile them into an organization called the church and expect to make anything out of it? More pointedly, how was I supposed to build the church with this mix, this motley crew of people? This would only hinder the work I was called to: the work of building the church.

I have always been a local church guy. "The church is the hope of the world." "The church is the plan of God on planet earth." "The church is the vehicle to advance the kingdom on earth." I have believed this and preached this with all my heart. I knew all the church passages in the New Testament, and yet I missed one very simple but profoundly important, extremely liberating truth that was clearly delineated in perhaps the most important church passage in the Bible:

"But what about you?" he asked. "Who do you say I am?"

Simon Peter answered, "You are the Messiah, the Son of the living God."

Jesus replied, "Blessed are you, Simon son of Jonah, for this was not revealed to you by flesh and blood, but by my Father in heaven. And I tell you that you are Peter, and on this rock I will build my church, and the gates of Hades will not overcome it. I will give you the keys of the kingdom of heaven; whatever you bind on earth will be bound in heaven, and whatever you loose on earth will be loosed in heaven." (Matt. 16:15–19)

This passage is particularly important because it is the first time the word *church* is mentioned in the Bible. And the *principle of the first mention* teaches us that the ideas contained in the first mention of an idea will shape that idea throughout the rest of Scripture. There is a lot of cool stuff about the church in this passage, but I want to focus on one phrase: "I will build my church."

When I saw that, it hit me like a ton of bricks. I had been trying to build the wrong thing! It doesn't say "*you* will build my church." Nor does it say "I will build *your* church." Honestly, the latter is how I was viewing it. Sadly, most of my prayers were of this ilk: "Lord, help me out and hook a boy up here! I need more money. I need more people—better people, good people, people who can help me build. Come on, I'm just trying to do what You called me to do, build Your church."

In this passage, it was as if Jesus was saying to me, "I have an all-encompassing plan for My church. It will overcome darkness, liberating people from its deceiving power. I will rescue people from the power of sin. I will establish My reign on this planet, the kingdom of God, through My church, and it will sweep the globe. I will unleash the gospel through My people, and I will empower My church through the person of the Holy Spirit. I will build My church and I will be her head."

I believe in vision and planning and structure and all the other stuff that has to be there to make church a church. But if it's *my* church, then all that stuff starts with me, and I have to get the Lord to help me with it. However, if it's *His* church, then all that stuff starts with Him, and He enlists me to cooperate with Him. It's His vision, not my vision. It's His people, not my people. This is no small point, so don't miss it.

Sadly, I think many pastors and church leaders think of the people as *my* people and the vision as *my* vision and therefore the role of the people is to help *me* build *my* vision. I don't think our goal should be to build the church but to build the people and let Jesus build the church. Let me explain.

Grace, His divine enablement, is the fuel that enables us to walk with Him, individually and collectively. Grace comes from Jesus. The Holy Spirit empowers the church and has been sent to us by the Father and the Son. The gospel is the power of God for salvation. It doesn't contain the power of God, it *is* the power of God. Justification is a declaration by God that makes us righteous before Him and occurs when we put our faith in Him (which incidentally is a gift from God). All this comes from Him. It almost sounds like He doesn't need us at all!

But as we read the Bible, we see elders and leaders in the church—human infrastructure. And we see small groups and missions and authority in the church—systems infrastructure. As we read the New Testament, we see there is a lot of stuff that people can do in church as well. Why doesn't God just do it all?

Because sanctification—the process of becoming like Jesus, the process of life change, the process of discovering our purpose—is a cooperative process. To grow into His likeness, we cooperate with His operations in our lives. We read the Word, worship, and fast and pray. We participate in the sacraments. We obey the leadership of the Holy Spirit in our lives and use our gifts to help others.

Others in the body use their gifts to help us. We repent when we sin and we exercise our faith to reach beyond the natural to experience His provision in our lives. And we work together and seek to get along with one another, which requires us to embrace the cross, which in turn enables us to change— into His likeness. All of this requires leadership and structure.

To discover who we really are and God's individual plan for our lives, we need to be in a local church with a huge, powerful vision. It is vision that draws us forward and empowers us to extend beyond our comfort zones. That vision empowers us to do things we never thought we could do.

Caution! Don't flip the script and get the idea that I am saying the leader gets his own vision and harnesses the human and financial resources of the people to make it happen. It isn't about the leader. It never was about the leader. It never will be about the leader. It will always and only be about Jesus and His people doing the unimaginable all over the world. How many times do we read these words in the Bible: "I will be their God and they shall be My people"? And what is the first thing God says when He reveals the New Jerusalem at the very end of time in Revelation 21:3? "They will be his people, and God himself will be with them and be their God."

From the very beginning, God's plan was to have a people for Himself. That plan did not change after the fall, but God did add one very important dimension to it. Part 1: "I will be their God and they will be My people. I will save them from sin and bring them to Myself." Part 2: "I will restore their brokenness, build them into a people called the church, and through them extend My kingdom all over the planet." Part 1 is the work God does to us. Part 2 is the work God does with us. Part 1: God does it all. Part 2: we cooperate with God.

As we read the New Testament, we find that God has called leaders—pastors, elders, deacons, parents, teachers, small group leaders, friends—to aid in the cooperative process of building people. The New Testament calls this *discipleship*. It is the impact of one life upon another, and it is a cooperative venture between believers. Leadership, followership, teaching, correction, accountability, friendship, sharing, participation, reconciliation, honoring, obedience—the list goes on. These are all cooperative acts and part of the sanctification, people-building process. Simply put, this is the work of the church: to build people (make disciples) and train them individually and as a group (the local church) to extend His kingdom everywhere we find ourselves and even in places where we are not welcome.

The Great Commission is found in five places in the New Testament (Matt. 28:18–20; Mark 16:15–18; Luke 24:44–49; John 20:19–23; Acts 1:8), but the most famous of these is Matthew 28:18–20:

> Then Jesus came to them and said, "All authority in heaven and on earth has been given to me. Therefore go and make disciples of all nations, baptizing them in the name of the Father and of the Son and of the Holy Spirit, and teaching them to obey everything I have commanded you. And surely I am with you always, to the very end of the age."

In the Greek, there are three participles and one imperative in this section of Scripture:

Participle #1: going
Participle #2: baptizing
Participle #3: teaching
Imperative: make disciples

Why is this important? The only true imperative (command) in this most famous rendering of the Great Commission is to "make disciples." It's a people-building command, and the three participles are part of the process of how that is to be done.

Go to the people in the world around you with the gospel, and I will bring them into relationship with Me. *Baptize* those who come into relationship with Me in the name of the Father and of the Son and of the Holy Spirit and help them start a new life: new passions, new values, new family, new perspective, and new allegiances. *Teach* them everything I taught you about how to walk with Me, how to find your place in the body of Christ, and how to use your gifts and callings to cooperatively advance My kingdom.

The command was not to build a ministry or an organizational structure called church but to build people, and as Jesus promised in Matthew 16:18, He would build them into a world-changing organism called the church—or more particularly, "My church."

Jesus is saying, "You help Me build My people, and I will build My church." If we focus on building the church (the organization), we will always be short of what we feel we need: not enough people, not enough money, not enough leaders. If, on the other hand, we focus on building the people He sends our way, everything else will fall into place. Though there may be ups and downs, struggle and difficulty in the process, He will make good on His promise to build His church.

This is so liberating. If we discover His vision for the particular church we lead and concentrate on helping people become like Him—think like Him, pray like Him, forgive like Him, obey like Him, serve like Him, love people like Him, give of ourselves like Him, yearn to advance the kingdom like Him—He will build the church.

The job is building people. If we concentrate on that (and that is what leadership development is all about), God will use them to do amazing things!

A HANDCRAFTED PURPOSE

We lost a lot in the fall in the garden of Eden. Sin separated us from God eternally and we died spiritually. From that point forward, trouble and stress, sickness and death, tribulation and tragedy have always been a part of life in the human race. And when God put Adam and Eve out of the garden, we were cut off from His presence and, as a consequence, lost our sense of belonging. In addition, when we were separated from the Person who was our creator, we lost touch with our purpose, not just as the human race, but as individuals as well.

Thus every human being is plagued with two basic questions: Where do I belong? Do I count? We crave a place to belong and the knowledge that we are significant. We feel alone and, in reality, in many ways we are. All of us will one day be required to stand alone before the Holy One and account for our sins. (Thank God, Jesus is our mediator!) And since sin has cut us off from our Creator, our understanding of our purpose and who we were made to be has been twisted and distorted.

Jesus came to restore our connection and fellowship with God. Once we come to know Him, we find we are immediately included in the company of those whom He calls the church, and we have fellowship with others who have also been redeemed. (Of course, learning how to get along and build one another up is part of the discipleship process we talked about earlier.) Once we are a part of this life-giving fellowship, we are in position to begin to discover why we are here on earth in the first place. But we can't discover this on our own for several reasons. For instance, we were not made to be alone, so who we are as individuals is inextricably tied to other people. Who we are and why we are here can only be discovered in community with others.

In a way, every church is an orchestra, each with its own music (calling and vision) and a set of gifted musicians. As new members are added to the orchestra, the band must flex, make room for them, and be patient as the new members struggle to find which instrument they are called and gifted to play. One truth is consistent, however: no matter how weak or proficient the players are, the parts they play in the score only make sense in concert with the other performers. A score is made up of a seemingly infinite number of notes; some may get to play only a few notes, but each is important if the music is going to find its true voice. When we recognize that truth, yield to the leadership of the heavenly conductor, and gratefully receive mentorship from the more mature members, the band improves as the players develop their gifts and find their fit and purpose.

The passion to build people begins with the realization that each one has a unique calling and a set of gifts that match that calling. Each person has a purpose. That notion is quickly followed by the idea that it is the role of the church and its leaders—per the calling of its leaders—to help people discover their purpose. Indeed, this is in the best interests of the leaders and the church itself since the music can never be all that God intended it to be without all the musicians playing their parts.

Perhaps no passage of Scripture is clearer on this point than Ephesians 4:1. First, writing to church members, not only to church leaders, Paul exhorts them in verse one to "live a life worthy of the calling you have received." Another translation phrases it as an appeal to "walk in a manner worthy of the calling to which you have been called" (ESV). Most people think of calling in reference to those who make their living in vocational ministry, but here Paul is addressing believers in general. Everyone is called. And it is a God-ordained (He does the calling) and magnificent call. Believers are instructed to live a life worthy of it. They play an important part in the orchestra.

Then Paul gives the reason that God places leaders in the body in the first place: to make more leaders, to equip them to do ministry, to empower them to use what God gave them. In verses 11 and 12 Paul says, "So Christ himself gave the apostles, the prophets, the evangelists, the pastors and teachers, to equip his people for works of service, so that the body of Christ may be built up." God gave leaders to the people to prepare them; other translations use the verb "equip."

Notice what happens when leaders focus on building people: the body is built up! Jesus works through people to build other people. This creates a leadership development incubator. Look at verses 13–16:

> Until we all reach unity in the faith and in the knowledge of the Son of God and become mature, attaining to the whole measure of the fullness of Christ.
>
> Then we will no longer be infants, tossed back and forth by the waves, and blown here and there by every wind of teaching and by the cunning and craftiness of people in their deceitful scheming. Instead, speaking the truth in love, we will grow to become in every respect the mature body of him who is the head, that is, Christ. From him the whole body, joined and held together by every supporting ligament, grows and builds itself up in love, as each part does its work.

Notice that as people are built and empowered to operate in their calling as they discover their purpose, growth is the result. People grow as individuals, and as they grow, they operate more effectively in their calling, and as a result, the church grows. I love that last line: "grows and builds itself up in love, as each part does its work." It's a beautiful cycle—growth begets growth. And how did this glorious process get started in the first place? Go back to verses 11 and 12. The leaders whom God put in the church made building, equipping, and empowering people their focus. And what is the result? Jesus, through His people, builds the church.

Every person is handcrafted by God, fashioned with a purpose, His purpose. Inside each one is a champion clawing to get out. Our job is to help that champion find expression through them. Over the years I have discovered there are five truths that inform a people-building mind-set.

1. People Grow Best in a Grace-Filled Environment Where Failure Is Not Fatal

When you read this, you could be tempted to think, *Hey, this guy is giving people a free pass to sin!* Nothing could be further from the truth. In fact, I am not talking about sin at all. I am talking about giving people space to discover who God made them to be, to experiment with their gifts and callings, and in that context, to fail without fear of reprisal.

Of all organizations on the planet, the church should be the most grace-filled. After all, we are recipients of grace. Everything we have and everything we are have come to us by and through grace, and the more we mature, the more convinced we are of that reality. It just makes sense that we would treat one another with grace. And yet it seems the church is in a perpetual struggle to make room for one another. I think it goes back to the root of religion. Let me explain.

Christianity was not designed to be another religion; it was designed to be a relationship with God—a God who rescued us from sin, whose incomprehensible mercy swept away our sins through the sacrifice of His own Son, and who, through amazing grace, declares us to be the righteousness of God in Christ. Religion, on the other hand, focuses not on relationship but on performance. Christianity operates from the inside out. Religion operates from the outside in. Christianity supposes that once the heart changes (inside), the outward life will reflect that change through upgraded behavior (outside). Religion presumes that conformity to certain behaviors (outside) will somehow magically transform the heart to match (inside). Christianity is about the continual conversion of the heart. Religion is about outward compliance and conformity. Grace powers Christianity. Comparison powers religion. And because of our fallen nature, the church is in love with the idea of comparisons.

We come by that propensity naturally, and it is reinforced at times by our leaders. If building the organization of the church is our focus and people our resource, then comparison is a natural outgrowth of that. Whoever has the biggest church must be the most spiritual or at least the most successful pastor. If, however, building people is the focus, comparison has no place, because life change is impossible to measure since it originates from the heart—inside out.

Before we coach people to step outside their comfort zone and try new things in an effort to discover who they are,

we must first create an environment where failure is not fatal.
People have to believe they are operating in a judgment-free
zone, a place where attempts at ministry that end in failure draw coaching, not criticism, out of their mentors. This
begins with honesty on the part of leaders. The people up
front must be willing to be transparent about the lessons they
have learned and are learning, not only through their successes, but also through their less-than-savory ministry and
life experiences. The idea is that we're all on a journey, and
we're all being shaped by a God who loves us. He is completely
committed to forming Christ in us, which means He uses
both our successes *and* failures to shape us into the people He
created us to be. We're all in this together, so join the journey.

2. The Church Should Be a Permission-Granting Institution

You're never really ready. You may have thought you were,
but you weren't. Everyone is an expert at marriage until they
get married. You weren't ready, but it was the right time, and
you learned along the way through many mountains and
many valleys. Everyone judges the lack of child-rearing prow-
ess among young parents until they have their first kid. You
thought you were ready, but you weren't. And yet, in the economy of God, having that first child was in His perfect timing,
and you learned about as much about life as the child did.

The same is true in almost every area of life, and it's especially true in church. But we tend to hold people back until

they're ready. I think being willing is a more valuable attribute than being ready. Ready is such a sliding scale. Was Gideon ready? Was Moses ready when he argued with God about his fear of public speaking? Was young David really ready, or was he passionately *willing* to lay his life down for the cause? Were Jesus's disciples ready? Would any of those guys have made it as elders in our churches when Jesus passed the baton to them after Calvary? Paul was well-trained, but was he really ready to go into the synagogue to preach less than one week after being born again? Gideon, Moses, David, the disciples, and Paul all turned out to be great, but none of them started there. None of them were ready, but all of them were willing.

And sometimes it takes an act of Congress to get permission to try something new! Someone says, "I'd like to do an outreach to the homeless." But his pastor says: "Well, you'll need to write up your suggestion and submit it to the outreach committee. If they approve it, we'll put it on the outreach calendar for next year." I know that is an extreme example, but you get the point. I believe in leadership and following the vision God has given for the local church, but I also believe every believer is connected directly to the head, who is Christ. The pastor is not the head of the church.

A better analogy for the pastor is coach. If there are a bunch of paid leaders on the staff, then think of the senior pastor as the head coach and all the other leaders as position coaches. Coaches aren't players; they don't take the field.

Players take the field and play the game. Let's get the coaches off the field and let the players play. Coaches are usually people who've played the game before, so they have insight and wisdom to pass along to help the players execute the game plan more effectively. Coaches know the team wins when the players play well, so their focus is player development. Pastors and staff know the church wins when the members walk in their calling and fulfill their purpose, thus leadership development—people building—is their focus. We are called to help the players play the positions God has called them to within the body of Christ. Let's get them on the field, not hold them back until—until what? Until they are ready? Who is ever really ready? Say yes, and then coach.

Pathways into ministry need to be easy to find in the local church. Everyone needs to know what their next step is. A well-defined leadership-development pipeline will help with that.

3. Religious Control Is a Form of Wickedness

Maybe it's just me, but I always thought it strange when, for instance, I went into a shoe store and a salesperson said, "I'm not carrying that line of shoe anymore" or "I'm going to put these on sale next week" or "I'm not open on that day." It sounded strange because it wasn't his shoe store; he only worked there. I wondered, *What is going on in his soul to prompt him to act like he is in a position that he clearly isn't?*

I would have been okay with "We don't carry that line any-more" or "We are going to put these on sale" or "We aren't open on that day."

The people in our churches do not belong to us, and I know it sounds like I'm arguing semantics, but we pastors should not call them "my people," because they aren't. I think that belies a deeper issue. "My church," "my ministry," "my people"—none of that is true. "You are not your own; you were bought at a price. Therefore honor God with your bodies" (1 Cor. 6:19–20). Jesus paid for us and we belong to Him; we pastors are only stewards of His people. What an amazing honor it is to be called by Jesus into a co-laboring relationship with Him to serve the people He draws into relationship with Him. The purpose of God-given leadership is to equip and empower His people to operate in their calling.

It follows that if the church is mine, then the people, who are the church, are also mine. But as I said earlier, Jesus clearly says, "I will build *My* church," not "the church" and especially not "your church." Whoever dies for them gets to have them. And when I look at the cross, I see only Jesus there.

Why is this important? This book is about creating a leadership-development culture in local churches, and *culture* is the key word. Later, I will make the case that language helps create culture and "my" is part of a language set that is pastor-centric, which is antithetical to a true leadership-development culture, which is actually people-centric.

On another front, some leaders confuse leadership with control. In their view, the "my way or the highway" form of leadership is simply part of being a strong leader. Actually, that is part of being a controlling leader. I have learned that if you lead people with an open hand, the people you lead will do everything they can to stay in your hand. But if you lead them with a closed fist, they will do everything they can to get out of your hand.

Strong leadership is exemplified by a crazy big vision and a radical belief in the people God has brought into the church family. Strong leadership is decisive and passionate about people. Jesus was passionate about people—He died for them. Control kills, but empowering leadership releases people into the plan of God for their lives. Simply put, leadership is always given for the benefit of those under that leadership.

4. Generosity Is the Default Mode

Generosity is the opposite of control. Generosity is more than giving away a lot of money. Generosity is a disposition of the heart. Generous people, people who are generous with their time, forgiveness, love, wisdom, finances, kindness, and joy, are well loved and never lack friends because they are others-oriented. On the other hand, stingy people hoard their personal and financial resources for themselves. They are slow to forgive and reticent to share. People are not attracted to them, and they make poor leaders, not because they lack talent, but because they kill the leadership-development culture.

In our church, we operate by the following axiom: In dealing with people, if you are going to err, always err on the side of generosity. Enough said.

5. Grace Is More than a Doctrine

Jesus made it clear that we should treat others the same way we have been treated. Think of all that Jesus has done for us! And all that He has done has been completely without regard to our condition, without regard to what we deserve. "He who did not spare his own Son, but gave him up for us all—how will he not also, along with him, graciously give us all things?" (Rom. 8:32). God's grace has been more than our help; it has been our lifeline. If God deals with us from the vantage point of grace, we must deal with others in the same way. Once again, grace does not mean being soft on sin. Grace without justice is not grace. Love *and* truth must exist together for either to remain balanced. Jesus is in the grace business and the people business. If we are to co-labor with Him and reflect His character, so must we be.

The call is *from* God, but it is a call *to* people—to love them, believe in them, and build them. For a leader in the church, that's the real job.

THE TRUMP CARD
THAT IS CULTURE

My parents were born in the 1920s and grew up in a generation when a complicated card game called bridge was popular
to play. When I was little, my parents hosted or attended
bridge parties at least a couple of times a month. Everyone
would dress up, get babysitters for their kids, and bring great
stuff to eat. Those parties were epic. Lots of talking and
laughter, and they took a lot of time. When Mom and Dad
hosted a bridge party, the four of us kids were sent to our
rooms to play, but I just *had* to sneak out to listen to what was
going on in the living room. While I never learned to play the
game, I did learn two very important things: (1) how to sneak

into the snacks while no one was looking (bridge is kind of a snobby game, so the snacks were always the best) and (2) the trump card is the most powerful card in the deck. No matter what card was played, no matter how powerful the card was, the trump card beat all. And when someone played a trump, it could be a game changer.

Every organization, no matter its size, has its own culture. Nations have distinct cultures. For example, Italian culture is different from Japanese culture (vastly different). Large companies have distinct cultures, even among companies in the same business. Apple is different from Samsung, even though they both produce smartphones. Families have distinct cultures, even families who reside in the same small town or live on the same street.

Culture is who we are and governs what we do and what we hold dear. Culture tells us what is good and right about life and what is wrong or offensive. Culture serves as a filter through which we view life, and therefore it shapes what we think, fuels our opinions, and informs our worldview. Culture determines what we celebrate and what we disdain. If we set out to change a nation or a company or a family or a church, we find it is impossible to do so without first changing the culture of the nation or company or family or church. Any attempt at change without first addressing the culture will meet with failure because culture is that powerful. It is the trump card.

Think about a family who moves to the United States

from the old country. In the first generation or two, the only thing that is different about that family is where they reside. Everything else stays pretty much the same. They import the celebrations, customs, and food choices from the old country. They reject the obvious conveniences and savings of shopping in modern grocery stores and prefer to shop instead in specialty shops that import foodstuffs from the old country.

Over time, the young people begin to assimilate into the culture in the new country. Their parents and grandparents are shocked and horrified at the defiance. "Where did you get these ideas?" "Why would you do this to us?" "What is this music?" "What is this food?" "Where did you get these clothes?" "If my mother could see this!" "In the old country we never would have . . ."

With more time, as more and more aspects of the culture of the new country are assimilated by the young, attitudes, opinions, perspectives begin to change. Why? The filter is changing. Over time, behaviors begin to change. Why? The rules are changing. The definitions of what is beloved and what is abhorrent begin to shift and broaden. Why? A culture shift is happening. And yet, at the same time, the first couple of immigrant generations continue to hold to old country values, old country behaviors, and old country perspectives, even though they live in a new country. Why? Their culture remains intact. They will not change, because their culture hasn't changed. Culture trumps all.

ONE VERY IMPORTANT FACT

This book is not about nations or companies or families; this book is about churches and, more particularly, about building better leaders faster in the context of the local church. And that is precisely why we have to talk about culture. Get this one thing straight: your church has a culture. If you planted the church, it started with you, maybe even before you, but you added to it. If you are a leader in a local church, that culture helped shape you and will dictate your future to some degree.

You may not realize it, and you may not be able to articulate the key components of it, but your church has a culture. It *already* has a culture. I have talked about leadership development all over the world and found, almost universally, that leaders tend to run right past the idea of culture, choosing rather to focus on building a pipeline to produce leaders. "Our culture is great" is how most leaders respond to the question of culture, and yet most leaders, honestly, do not even understand it.

In any organization, leaders shape the culture, and the culture shapes the people. We are all indebted to Samuel Chand's *Cracking Your Church's Culture Code* for outlining how culture works in an organization.[1] It actually trumps everything else! Church leaders desperately want better leaders faster, but they do not know how to build them because they have overlooked the power of culture.

The press today is for more volunteers in the church. In an effort to recruit more volunteers, leaders inadvertently build a volunteer culture, which is antithetical to a leadership-development culture. At the same time, they often tack a leadership pipeline program onto the church, hoping to build a better supply of leaders. Sadly, in the end, the predictable happens: culture trumps the program, and the pipeline fails to produce the desired results. We graduate people from the pipeline who know more about leadership than they did before, but they're often not better leaders. Leaders are naturally built and brought forth in a leadership—not a volunteer-oriented—culture.

Can you change a church's culture? Yes, but you have to understand it before you can change it. We'll get into the nuts and bolts of building a leadership-development pipeline, but first, let's give ourselves to understanding culture. Here are thirteen things I know about culture.

1. Culture equals the unique characteristics of a people.

These things apply to everyone in every setting in every era: nations, tribes, companies, families, baseball teams, choirs, churches. Definitions vary, but *culture*, in general, is made up of at least six things.

1. **Celebrations:** Every people group has a set of celebrations that help define who they are. In the United States, we celebrate the Fourth of July, Independence

Day. Think about American individualism in light of that celebration and you begin to see how powerful celebrations are in defining and creating culture. Imagine a Jewish family celebrating Shabbat or a Muslim making a once-in-a-lifetime pilgrimage to Mecca. Most rituals are less formal or have no connection to religion.

For years on Thanksgiving, our family had an annual soccer match we called the Thunderboot Classic. The story behind the thunderboot stems from my sister-in-law's ill-fated idea to actually wear boots to play the game when, in a burst of competitive passion, she kicked my wife's feet out from under her and then found herself falling headlong onto the turf as well. Both women lay there, laughing hilariously, sprawled out on the ground, pine straw in their hair. Thus the game was christened the Thunderboot Classic on the spot.

Celebrations include rituals and feasts, anything of a celebratory nature that is continually repeated. It could be happy or sad, but the ritual or the feast survives the test of time because it adds to or commemorates something that in some way defines a people.

2. **Superstitions and Fears:** These things can range from actual superstitions to things that simply force us to unite to survive. Some people groups may, because of a legend, fear a certain spirit, so they coalesce to protect

themselves. Others may fear the loss of freedoms, so they unite to fight for their rights or defend themselves from the threatened loss of them. In recent times, nations have found themselves in a place of heightened unity because of a collective fear of terrorism. People are willing to give up some freedoms at airports, for example, in an effort to preserve their way of life. Superstition and fear are powerful cultural tools. Think of the power of the underground church in history and around the world today, which is derived in part from the unity created by the fear of persecution.

3. **Ideologies**: Every group has a collection of commonly held beliefs. The National Rifle Association is held together by the Second Amendment of the US Constitution: the right to bear arms. The commonly held beliefs of other groups may be more subtle and nuanced. Employees at a particular publishing company may feel loyal to that company for its passion to help artists find their voice. Being there for the artist is part of that company's flavor or culture.

4. **Rules**: Each culture has a set of written or, more often, unwritten rules that define how they choose to live. These rules comprise the code of what is right and what is wrong. The types of laws a nation or municipality make, along with the types of penalties associated with violation of these laws, illuminate the values of

the people who reside there. Analysis of those laws can reveal a slant toward or away from religious freedom, racism, or despotism of which the framers of those laws may not even have been aware.

In a much smaller context, a new employee may not be aware of an unwritten rule (that everyone one else knows) that no one bothers the boss on Mondays until he has had his second cup of coffee. In fact, in every group of any size, most cultural infractions occur in the land of unwritten rules. It might be good to consider how many unwritten rules are in play in our churches and on our staffs and how they came to be. Ask what values they reveal. The purveyors of those rules are often the last to recognize the values they reveal but the first to defend obedience to them.

5. **Celebrities:** Our heroes are those who did the most to push our values forward, often at great price or sacrifice. We love our heroes and the great stories that accompany them. A drive through any city in any country will reveal a lot about the culture of that people. Our heroes protect us from our fears. Our heroes embody our ideologies. We sometimes build celebrations around our heroes, and there are lessons to be learned from their lives, real or imagined, that underscore the rules by which we live. The telling of these microhistories, these often-exaggerated biographies, conveys

powerful culture-building ideas. They underscore our fears. They teach *how we live* (as opposed to *how they live*). They move us to celebrate. And they show us what life is all about. In other words, these stories reveal our culture, which in turn shapes our worldview.

6. **Actions:** A culture is not a culture until it manifests itself in our actions or in a set of behaviors that are unique to us. "This is how we do it." When culture begins to take shape through action, that culture has been established in the community.

Many a leader has preached a sermon or a series to define a culture for the congregants, but they're unaware this never works. You *already* have a culture. When you start something new, as in planting a new church, you can tell people what you *want* the culture to be. But once a group has become a group and begins to act and operate together, the culture of that group is revealed through what is valued enough to celebrate, what causes fear and concern, what it believes by how it functions, what rules are written down and what rules are unwritten, and who it honors as heroes. Finally, all these values find expression through our actions.

As a church leader, think about the following:

- What do we celebrate and what does *how* we celebrate reveal about who we are? Discounting the obvious (Easter,

Christmas, etc.), what do you celebrate? Attendance records? People's stories of life change? Meeting financial goals? Honestly, it all goes back to what you count and what makes you cry. People will become what you celebrate.

- What are we or what are our people afraid of? What suspicions do we carry toward other churches, toward the government, or toward other religions?

- What do we functionally believe? What truths do we hear expressed in our people's language? Are we religious in a negative way? Are we grace-filled in action toward others?

- What is our unwritten code? New people pick up on this quickly. Are we open and inviting or are we restricted and eager to protect what we have? What do we believe about people? Is it a value to believe more for others than they believe for themselves?

- Who are our heroes and why? What and who do we honor? Are our guest speakers our heroes? Are church members who overcome the odds and break through in some area of their lives our heroes? Are the only stories we tell of people who have it all together? Two things drive every person: they want to belong and they want to feel significant. The stories you elevate tell people how they can belong and illuminate the pathway to significance.

- Actions make culture permanent. What are the "we do it this way" actions that are particular to your church?

If all the above reveal a slant toward making a big deal about people, their growth, and their development within the context of a grace-filled environment, you are well on your way to developing a leadership-development culture.

2. A church's culture is how the church feels and how outsiders feel when they are there.

A church has a personality just as a person does. Some people are cold and distant while others are warm and friendly. Some people are aggressive and determined while others may be more whimsical and passive. Some people are outgoing and gregarious while others may be more reserved and shy. Similarly, churches can be quiet, intellectual, polite, and reserved. Churches can be casual, fun, exciting, and inspiring. Churches can be boring, angry, and even mean.

In many ways, the culture of a church is the personality of the church, and people pick up on that personality, that culture, as soon as they walk in the door. If your culture, your church's personality, is about people—connecting people to God, serving people, helping people, building people, celebrating what God is doing in the lives of people—that will come through and scream to your guests, "You are welcome and wanted here. We are honored to have you and we want you to stay."

Some people might say, "Our church is about God," and that's great, but don't forget that God is about people. He sent His only Son to die for them, and even now His Son is preparing a place for them. He said so Himself: "I go and prepare a place for you, I will come back and take you to be with me that you also may be where I am" (John 14:3).

At the end of the day, the leader of a church is the chief culture creator for that church. He defines its DNA, namely, the spiritual genetic imprint the church has on the people who come into its orbit. The closer people come to the center of the church—or said another way, the closer people come to the core of the church—the stronger the genetic stamp. In other words, these people have assimilated with the culture and are now disseminating it.

3. Language creates and carries culture.

Like every generation or era, the culture of the 1960s was expressed through its unique language. This was a time defined by the Vietnam War, the civil rights movement, the sexual revolution, the Cold War, and "sex, drugs, and rock 'n' roll," and its language reflected that. People chanted "Make love, not war" during protests in the streets. Kids' vocabularies were spiced with words like *groovy* and *cool*. Formerly "busted" meant someone broke something, but in the sixties, "busted" came to mean someone was arrested for possession of illegal drugs. People called one another "man." "Hey, man, you got the time?" "Man, we gotta get out of here!" And a cat wasn't a feline animal but a guy, a male person. "Man, that cat could play the bass!" The language defined the culture and helped make it portable, that is, it carried the culture to other people.

The same is true of the 1970s, an era that saw massive growth in the music genres of both rock and rhythm and blues. Disco broke onto the musical scene as well, and every kid wanted a lava lamp, because it made his or her room feel more psychedelic. Kids used words like *bogart*, not as the last name of a favorite actor, but as in "push your weight around." Words and phrases such as *funky, to the max, catch you on the flip side* ("see you when it's over"), *right on*, and *chump* (it was never good to be called a chump) were en vogue. The language fit the culture, reflected its values, and also shaped the culture into what it became.

The same could be said of every generation up to the present. How many words have been created in the Internet era (including the word *Internet*) and have shaped culture as they sought to give understanding of the massive advances in technology?

Language shapes culture. It creates it because it gives expression to the ideas and concepts that reflect our values. People may not always "walk the talk," but they always "talk the walk." In other words, people don't always live out what they say their values are, but they always reveal their values and their culture through their language.

Language carries or spreads culture to everyone in an organization. In fact, language can actually determine who in the organization is truly in and who is truly out. Those who understand and use the language understand the ideas the words are meant to convey. They are in, and those who don't are out. Grasping the language of a church is far more important and powerful than simply joining it. And that reveals an important leadership lesson.

Promoting people to places of prominence in the local church based on potential, charisma, or skill before they are fully assimilated into the culture can be dangerous for the organization, especially if the individual is a strong leader. Why? Because they carry a culture too, and without realizing it, they will infuse their culture into yours, thus, to some degree, defusing your culture and causing confusion in the ranks. Author Larry Osborne said, "Don't let the conversation down the hall trump the vision on the wall." In short, language carries culture.

4. Change the language, change the culture.

In order to change an organization, we must first shift the culture. And to do that, leaders must change the language. Believe me, it sounds much easier than it is. Leaders can't simply stand up and say, "This is now what we believe about our future" and expect everyone to get it.

Now, shaping culture in a new or young organization is much easier, because the leader gets to define a new set of words at the outset. The process in a young organization is *say* then *show*. Teach the people the concepts, using the desired language, and then lead the people into an experience of that truth. First comes teaching and then comes action. For example, one can teach on mission, and then lead an outreach in practical, hands-on service to the community.

It is much harder, however, to change the culture in a mature organization, because the terms are already defined, a language has already been crafted. A culture already exists with a language that supports it. The process in a mature organization is *show* then *say*. Lead the people into an experience and then talk about it afterward, teach them what the experience means. In the example above, we talked about the word *mission*. That word in some mature churches might mean a professional, seminary-trained person who lives among and serves people in a foreign land. In most cases, they have come by that definition honestly in that the church itself may have a history of sending highly trained people to live and serve in other parts of the world. So lead an outreach, for example, in practical, hands-on service to the community, and then follow up that experience in the weeks to come with teaching on mission, redefining the word to mean the call to every believer to impact their world.

To change the culture of a church, you must change the language. It is a slow process, like turning a large ship, but with patience, it can be done.

5. Culture must be backed by action for it to stick.

Your culture determines behaviors, and behaviors make the culture permanent. Said another way, your culture determines what you do, and what you do gives life to your culture.

Consider the six elements of culture in our leadership-development culture. How would we use action to empower a new culture?

1. **Celebrations:** We hold three primary celebrations every year: one to reveal our yearlong, multifaceted outreach strategy and two SERVE team celebrations. Our SERVE team (which I will define in the next chapter) is not another name for a volunteer team; it is part of our leadership-development process, and the word *serve* is actually an acronym for our definition of leadership (which we stole from Chick-fil-A). Our SERVE team is comprised of everyone who leads worship on a stage, leads a small group, operates on a hospitality team or VIP team, leads outreaches, leads children's small groups, serves in the parking lot, and the list goes on. We call them leaders. We celebrate leadership and leaders in two huge fun events every year.

2. **Superstitions and Fear:** It is ungodly and unbiblical to use fear and superstition as a motivator, and we don't do it. The point here is that we all have fears that drive certain behaviors in our lives, and those fears, if properly understood, can and will promote culture. As I will describe later in this section and more fully in chapter 6, we do not use mass recruitment to fuel the ranks of our SERVE teams. There are no sermons on "you need to serve" followed by a mass recruitment.

There is no connection booth in the foyer (which in most settings is really just a "we need volunteers" booth). We do not pass clipboards, hand out cards, send mass or targeted emails, or send snail-mail invitations to a night with the pastor (so I can get you to volunteer). We don't do anything like that. Ever. Period. We only and always use a leadership skill we call *shoulder tapping* to invite people into ministry (I'll explain this fully in chapter 6). The fear would simply be, "If I do not continue to grow as a leader and if I do not continue to improve in the skill of shoulder tapping, I will fall behind in my lane and the overall mission will suffer." For us, leader is not a position people hold; it is who they are and what they do.

3. **Ideologies**: For us, building people *is* the job, not just building the organization. So engaging and developing others through shoulder tapping and our growth track (which is our leadership-development pipeline) is the role of every leader. We believe every person was created on purpose for a purpose, so helping him or her take his or her next step on that journey is crucial. Every leader at every level needs to be able to answer the question, "Who are you developing?" If you hold a leadership position and no one is following you, you aren't a leader.

4. **Rules (Written and Unwritten)**: Our growth track is more than an orientation to volunteerism. It is a

series of small groups designed to help people find and walk in their calling, but more particularly, it is our culture-creation mechanism (I'll fully describe this in chapter 7). Consequently we have written the rules down in the third component of the growth track under a section titled "Twelve Operational Principles." These are the rules. They describe why we do what we do and the way we do it. These aren't rules as in "rules to follow in order to be right with God"; these rules are statements that convey ideas that communicate the key elements of our culture. We have made a conscious attempt to remove all the guesswork from our culture by eliminating, as much as possible, the unwritten rules. The twelve operational principles inform our actions and behaviors.

5. **Celebrities:** The heroes in our church are the members who take their next steps in their journey toward their calling and purpose. These are the real heroes, the people who step outside their comfort zones, take a risk, face their fears, and attempt to make a difference in the lives of others. This is one of the things that makes us cry and, I believe, makes heaven cheer. God loves to do extraordinary things through ordinary people. It demonstrates His grace, power, and greatness. The heroes in our church are not the pastors (we're just the coaches); it's the people, because

they're the real players on the field. And so we tell their stories. We make videos of their stories and show them in our church services. We use their stories in sermons, sometimes with and sometimes without names, depending on their story and their comfort level. Recently, we passed out cards with photos and life-changing stories from our members. We enlarged them into posters and placed them all along the walls.

In some ecclesiastical situations, the heroes are the pastors and their pastor friends, which is fine. But you'll never build a leadership-development culture that way. God's people weren't made to sit in the stands and watch professional Christians play. God made His people for greatness. In my opinion, the coaches need to get off the field and let the players play. And then the coaches should celebrate everything they do right to advance the kingdom ball down the field.

6. **Actions**: Once again, actions make culture permanent. They give feet and hands to ideas. You know you have a leadership-development culture when the process of making leaders—otherwise known as discipleship—is happening in the church on its own. Then, and only then, can you be certain the values have taken hold and the culture you desire to form is taking shape.

Discipleship (or leader making) is obedience-based, not knowledge-based. This means that becoming a disciple or a leader is not simply learning the basic ideas of the Christian faith. It isn't just theology. It includes theology, but it goes beyond theology into practice. In chapter 2 we looked at the Great Commission and noted the three participles and one command in Matthew 28:18–20:

Participle #1: going
Participle #2: baptizing
Participle #3: teaching
Imperative: making disciples

The one command is a "do" command, not a "know" command. Culture building and leader making (discipleship) require action. Note that even the third participle, which is teaching, isn't teaching them to know; it's teaching them to do, more particularly, teaching them to obey.

> Then Jesus came to them and said, "All authority in heaven and on earth has been given to me. Therefore go and make disciples of all nations, baptizing them in the name of the Father and of the Son and of the Holy Spirit, and *teaching them to obey* everything I have commanded you. And surely I am with you always, to the very end of the age." (emphasis added)

If you want to build a leadership-development culture, one that sticks, actions must follow language. If language creates culture, then actions make culture permanent.

6. Culture trumps vision.

I love vision. Every leader does, because it's how leaders are made. Leaders see the future and are irresistibly drawn to it. That's why leaders love to preach about vision, so they can lead others into seeing the future. But vision leaks. People hear it, get it, give to it, clap for it, and then promptly forget it. I hate that, but it's true. And once vision has leaked, what do you do? What is left? Culture.

Vision is like a picture; it must be shown to people from time to time. People need to be reminded to look at it. And vision can change. It can be adjusted or altogether scrapped and replaced by an incoming leader. But culture *just is,* and every organization has one. As I said before, culture is like a person's personality; it's who he or she is. Culture is like the smell in a house. Every house has one, some good, some bad. It's the way a church feels. Vision leaks, but culture is ever present. It is who we are as a church family. And that's why culture will always trump vision.

It's a law. Left alone, without pressure, everything reverts to form. Without pressure, everything will revert to its original state, like an untended yard or garden. It you don't intentionally take care of that garden, it'll be a mess before you know it. You can make your garage immaculate, but if you don't watch it, it will return to the mess it was before. Why is that?

We always shift back to behaviors (actions) that we feel are normal, even if we know they are wrong. You put the lawn mower back where you always put it, as well as the shears, the trimmer, the garbage can, the toys, the . . . , and the . . . , and then the garage looks like it did before you cleaned it up. We shift back to the behaviors that feel normal. And what determines those behaviors? Culture!

Every family has a culture, and when the kids leave home and get married, the young couple fights to see whose family culture will dominate. Often there are compromises that follow, and the couple creates a hybrid or third culture that encompasses what they collectively see as the most savory aspects of their original cultures. Then later they tell their kids, "This is the way *we* do it!"

Culture determines behavior. It is who we are. It determines what we do and how we see the world, and because of that, culture trumps vision.

7. Culture can empower vision if both are aligned and share a common language.

This idea is simple but profound, and it underscores why it is so important for us to understand how culture works. If you have a strong prayer culture and you preach on vision, people in your church will naturally gravitate to prayer. If you have a strong outreach culture and you preach on vision, people will naturally interpret that vision through the lens of outreach.

Make sure your culture and your vision are aligned. If your culture is inward focused and your vision is outward focused, you are working against the grain of your culture, and in the end, your culture will win the day. Without pressure, everything reverts to form. But if your culture and vision are aligned, you release the exponential power of culture behind your vision.

If you preach your vision in the language of your culture, people automatically gravitate toward it. Remember, culture is who we are. It's what's normal, and we always shift toward behaviors we feel are normal. When you preach your vision in the language of your culture, people believe "This is us! Of course, I'm in!" I believe this is one reason why some churches always seem to move forward while others seem to get stuck in an oscillating cycle of starts and stops, never able to gain any consistent momentum. Alignment between culture and vision is powerful!

8. Culture can kill.

To create a toxic culture, leaders lead with or lead out of the following: religion, legalism, insecurity, control, manipulation, micromanagement, classism (the unbiblical idea that leaders are higher in rank and importance than the members), or management by fear. This type of environment is programmed to keep people small.

9. Culture can empower.

To create a life-giving culture, leaders lead with or out of the following: believing more for others than others do for themselves, forgiveness, generosity, creating an environment where failure is not fatal, high (but clear) expectations, shared wins, honor, focused vision, clarity on the win. This type of environment is designed to make people big.

By the way, honor is not just a bottom-to-top operation where people who are perceived as under, honor people who are viewed as over. In fact, the most powerful type of honor is the honor given by those who are over to those who follow them. If a leader expects those who follow to honor him, and yet he is stingy in giving honor to those he leads, he is insecure.

10. Culture passes from generation to generation if the core concepts are inculcated in the language of the next generation and the torch of leadership is passed to the children of the house.

I hope the idea that culture is carried and passed through language has been well established in this chapter, but the key to this point is found in identifying the children, the sons and daughters, of the house. These are people of the next generation who live the culture of the house. They have your heart and you have theirs. Honestly, in a church a leadership-development culture, they are not hard to find. In fact, they're everywhere, but what do they look like? Here are ten characteristics of a son or daughter of the house.

- They speak the language and actually listen to the words they use.
- They embrace the vision. For them, the vision is normal, not exceptional.
- They live the vision. They actually do what they say and not just talk about it.
- They repel attacks because the vision is personal to them. A criticism of the vision, in their minds, is an attack on them. Of course, every seasoned leader knows God allows criticism to refine the vision.
- They champion the values and help others to understand the culture.
- They honor the leaders and are worthy of honor themselves.
- They emulate the leaders. Imitation is not weakness; it's a sign of being a team player.
- They willingly sacrifice. They think the vision is worth it.
- They have a *we* rather than a *me* attitude. They are more for the team than they are for themselves.

- They give to the house so they can fulfill the vision. They do whatever it takes to make it happen.

11. Culture creates the "we" and preserves unity.

That is the nature of culture; it's who we are. Newcomers may not be able to describe what they feel when they get around it, but they can feel it. And if *it* is life-giving, it is attractive to them. It draws them in. We've all been in environments where, right from the start, we were attracted, drawn in, put off, or repelled.

Vision: Where are we going?
Strategy: How are we going to do it?
Mission: Why are we going?
Culture: Who are we?

The apostle Paul told us to "make every effort to keep the unity of the Spirit through the bond of peace" (Eph. 4:3). Culture does that for us. It preserves unity because it creates the "we." The family feeling in a church (for good or bad, either toxic or life-giving) is the presence of culture.

12. Slow is fast.

Building or shifting a culture happens slowly, but once you've been at it for a while, you begin to build momentum and the culture begins to rebuild itself. People begin to get it and speak the language. Once others begin to live and speak the values, your culture has begun to become self-authenticating.

Here's what I mean. When culture comes only from the leader, people watch and listen with an air of skepticism. But once they see and hear others doing and saying the same things, then the feeling is that everybody gets this and it takes off on its own.

Charisma and competency can be gained in a microwave, but character grows in a Crock-Pot. Building people also happens slowly, which means that building a leadership-development culture will take work and time. Be patient. Again, once others begin to say and do the same things, the culture begins to build itself. Here are four key "slow is fast" ideas to help build a leadership-development culture:

- People become what you celebrate. Be careful to never celebrate anything that cuts across or runs counter to your culture.
- Tell stories, lots of stories. Despite the fact that most people can read, every people group in every generation is oral at heart. We love a good story. Stories are how we make vision come alive and add to the lore of our culture.
- Let leaders live it before they tell it. People follow and imitate what their leaders do. You can't just tell people what your culture is; you demonstrate it first. People get tired of words; they want to see something.

- In life, variety is the spice of life and boring is bad. In culture building, consistency is king even if it feels boring. Say and show it until you can't stand saying it, and then the people are really just starting to get it.

13. Promote only culture carriers.

I've heard people say a leader must watch out for people in their organizations who carry a different vision because two visions equal division. And that's true. But more dangerous to your organization than a person with a different vision is a person with a different culture. And the sad truth is, the stronger a leader that person is, the more damage they are likely to do, and honestly it isn't their fault. You promoted them before they had your culture, and so they led, people followed, and it created a mess. In the end, they ended up leaving because the culture drove them out, but after they left, most pastors tend to view the poor soul as a rebel. In reality, they were probably great but were promoted before they embraced the culture.

Your best leaders may not be your strongest leaders. Your best leaders are your culture carriers. They're sneezers. When they sneeze, other people catch the germ. Bottom line, they spread your culture. They love your culture. They live your culture. They carry your culture. Hire those people! When people hear the same things from multiple sources, it increases credibility and endorses the culture in the minds and hearts of those who hear.

CHICK-FIL-A AND THE
END OF VOLUNTEERS
AT MANNA CHURCH

I was on the front row, taking notes as fast I could, at a Leadership Network Rapid Growth Learning Community in Dallas, along with a number of other leadership teams from great churches around the country. The guest was Mark Miller, vice president for leadership development at Chick-fil-A, and he was there to talk about Chick-fil-A's journey toward building a leadership culture at one of America's most successful fast-food chains. He chronicled the story in the book *The Secret: What Great Leaders Know and Do.*[1]

Because of its rapid growth, the company found itself in a place where it needed to build better leaders faster within the Chick-fil-A family. So they commissioned a team of leaders inside the company to study the problem. At the end of their extensive study, they found themselves in a place of exasperation. They had discovered there are about six thousand definitions of *leader* in use today. Even more exasperating, when they asked, "What do leaders do?" they found there are about 1,234 different actions! How were they to go back to upper management and explain that to build the leadership culture they were looking for, Chick-fil-A would have to train their people in 1,234 separate leadership actions?[2]

And then someone in their midst said, "Why don't we simply go back to the best leader on earth and do what He did?" The best leader he was referring to was Jesus, and what He did was serve. Right then, the SERVE model of leadership was born.[3]

Jesus taught that the greatest among us—the leader—is one who serves. Consider His words in Luke 22:24–27 (esv):

> A dispute also arose among them, as to which of them was to be regarded as the greatest. And he said to them, "The kings of the Gentiles exercise lordship over them, and those in authority over them are called benefactors. But not so with you. Rather, let the greatest among you become as the youngest, and the leader as one who serves. For who is the

greater, one who reclines at table or one who serves? Is it not the one who reclines at table? But I am among you as the one who serves."

In debunking the lordship model of leadership, which is sadly still functionally en vogue in many sectors of the church today, Jesus opened the leadership door to everyone who is willing to serve. He pushed aside the "follow me and make my dreams come true" authoritarian style of leadership and made way for a style of leadership designed to make other people great.

Once Chick-fil-A embraced this concept, it built a functional definition of leadership based on five key actions and used the word *serve* as an acronym for them.[4]

1. See the future
2. Engage and develop others
3. Reinvent continually
4. Value relationships and results
5. Embody the values

Borrowing from Chick-fil-A's SERVE model, Manna Church jettisoned a volunteer vocabulary and built a SERVE team model that allows people to serve in ministry while they are being developed into the leaders they were called to be. Mark Miller's presentation helped us to see that we had several problems we needed to address.

THE LANGUAGE ISSUE

First, we had a language issue. We already had a fairly strong leadership-development culture, but what we did not realize at the time was how much we were actually hurting ourselves with our language. We called people volunteers. By the nature of the word, a volunteer, in the minds of most, is not a leader. A volunteer is simply an unpaid person who fills a slot. For volunteers, the slot they fill is not personal, does not inform their identity, and has absolutely nothing to do with personal development. It's simply a job at the local church. But if that person is a leader and is growing in his or her understanding of leadership, then the opposite is true.

1. It is personal. "God has called me to join Him on a journey, and for now, this is my assignment."
2. It speaks to personal identity. "God has called me to *be* His son or daughter, but He has also called me on purpose and for a purpose to *do* something in His kingdom."
3. It has everything to do with personal development. "My present role in the local church may not be my final calling, but it is being used by God to prepare me for that calling."

Language is so powerful in the creation of culture! It is amazing how shifting just one word can have such an empowering effect.

Today, we don't use the word *volunteer* to describe people who serve in the local church. We say these people are on our SERVE team, and we call them leaders even though, when they first join a team, they may not see themselves as such. We never use the word *volunteer* as a noun. Our culture won't allow it. I have been in meetings where a new person uses that word, and you can feel it in the room. It's like someone uttered a profanity. Someone usually speaks up and says, "You mean SERVE team member" and explains the difference to the new person. That's how language both creates and carries culture. It spreads it.

Once we got rid of that nasty little word, we recognized we had to draw a line in the sand on how people are recruited or brought into ministry. If people are just volunteers, people to fill slots, then mass calls for participation, sermons designed to increase volunteerism, and videos designed to make volunteering seem more attractive all make sense, because you're just looking for people, any people, it doesn't matter who, to volunteer. *But* if people are leaders, then they need to be selected or shoulder tapped. (Please don't jump ahead to read that upcoming chapter.)

THE DEFINITION PROBLEM

The second issue, I am ashamed to say, was our definition of leadership; namely, we didn't have one. How embarrassing.

Here we had this growing leadership-development culture, and we didn't have a definition of what a leader is supposed to be. Sadly, if pressed, the best we could have come up with was, "A leader is a person who leads." I'm sure we could have jazzed it up with a bunch of cool John Maxwell stuff, but the truth is, the lack of a real definition left us without a way to tell people exactly what we wanted them to become. They had no idea what we were looking for. They had no idea what to aspire to. They had no idea if and when they had become a leader, because we had no idea what a leader really was!

But we were pretty clear on what a leader wasn't. A naturally autocratic person is not necessarily a leader, even though he likely sees himself that way. He's just a person who thinks everyone should see the world his way, and he's not ashamed to let them know it. A person with a position and a title is not necessarily a leader. We've all met the person who feels everyone should acknowledge his authority because of his title or position even though he carries no real authority in his personal life. He thinks authority goes with the title like fries go with a Happy Meal, but he doesn't understand that real authority is derived from a person's character. He's frustrated because people look right past him, and he's angry because they listen to and follow the quiet, humble, selfless person in the pack.

Being paid to do ministry doesn't even make anyone a leader. It just means they're getting a check. A leader, by definition, implies there are followers, and people don't follow a paycheck. People follow people. More particularly, they follow leaders. If no one is following you, then you're not a leader. I could go on and on. Somehow saying what a leader isn't is infinitely easier than saying what a leader is. Maybe that is why Chick-fil-A found more than six thousand definitions for the word *leader* in their study.

My guess is you don't have a definition of leader either. Come on. Be honest. What is a leader? That's a tough one, isn't it? And even if you do know what a leader is in your view, who else knows it? Does the pastoral staff at your local church know it? Do they share the same definition? But of much greater importance, do the people in your local church know what a leader is? Do they know what you expect of them? Do they know how to get there? How can they aspire to it? How can they work toward it if they don't know what it is?

Don't despair. We stole our definition and you can steal it too! That's why Mark Miller and Ken Blanchard wrote the book. Let me share with you how we applied the Chick-fil-A SERVE model in our local church. First, let me say I love that Miller and Blanchard did not take a theoretical approach to leadership in framing their definition. The idea here is not for people in our churches to pass a test on leadership. The idea is for them to do it! The goal is for them to become leaders.

Instead of a theoretical approach, Miller and Blanchard took a very practical slant by assigning actions to the five letters in the SERVE acronym. These are the five things leaders *do.* A person can look at this definition and see exactly what they are to do to become a leader. Here's our take on it.

- **See the future:** A leader is a person who sees where we as a church are going and how the ministry in which she serves fits into that future.[5] This is all about vision. How does the student ministry fit into the vision of the church? And what about the children's ministry? How about the prayer ministry or small groups or outreach? How do they fit in? What does the greeting team or the parking lot team have to do with what we are trying to do here? Leaders can answer those questions. They can see the future. Maybe the leader tells those on her team why the ministry they're involved in together is so important to the mission of the local church. Now she is leading. She's creating followership. She is pointing people in a clear direction because she is answering the why question. Why are we doing this? Why does this matter? Leaders see the future.

- **Engage and develop others:** In many ways, this is the real guts of the leadership definition. This is what it's all about. Engage means to get people involved, to invite them into ministry. In our context, this is shoulder tapping. (Don't jump ahead.) The skill here is in selecting the right people to make your ministry successful and in helping them see that joining you in that ministry is the next step in their journey. Developing others means to mentor them, to help them grow in their character and competency. Biblically this is called discipleship, but we have chosen to use the word *mentor*. We'll look at this in depth when we get into the details of building a leadership-development pipeline.

- **Reinvent continually:** Part of the leadership job is to improve the process. Leaders try to answer the following questions: How can we do this better? How can this ministry be more effective? How can we empower people to a greater degree? Since leaders see the future and how their ministry fits into the overall vision of the church, they are in the best position to suggest and make improvements to the operation of that ministry and to improve the process. Encouraging leaders to be creative and innovate accelerates their sense of ownership in the ministry they lead and enhances their buy-in with the overall vision of the church. "This is ours! We do this!" People naturally take pride in what they help create, and they tend to sacrificially support what they feel belongs to them. But this only works in an environment where failure is not fatal, an atmosphere where people can try, fail, and try again.

- **Value relationships and results:** The tendency is to see relationships and results at the opposite ends of the spectrum, and I think that is because most people naturally lean in one direction or the other. Simply put, some folks are people-oriented and others are task-oriented, but in church and in life, both teams and tasks are vital. People need to be in life-giving relationships in order to be healthy and develop properly, and the task adds purpose to the fellowship and helps the church accomplish its mission, or rather *our* mission. Rather than being antithetical, the two are complementary. One feeds the other. Working together on a task helps people establish relationships and develop crucial relational skills. Conversely, when people engage in ministry with others they consider as friends, the quality of that ministry exponentially increases. The joy of being together adds to the joy of doing the work, which translates into enhanced enthusiasm, passion, and drive. On top of that, seeing people having fun while serving on a team is attractive.

- **Embody the values:** Once we get the language right (the talk), then it's time to put those ideas into practice (the walk). And a leader is a person who walks the talk. Embodying the values includes two elements. First, she embraces the values. This is a heart issue. These aren't just the church's values; they become *her* values. This is where a leadership-development pipeline is essential. For us, our pipeline (which we call our *growth track*) is our culture-creating mechanism. It is the process through which our leaders are developed and our culture, our DNA, is disseminated throughout the congregation. Second, she puts the values into practice. This is the hand issue, the action stage. As I pointed out in chapter 3, this is where culture really takes hold, when ideas become actions. As leaders embrace the values internally and act out the values externally, they become culture carriers. As they interact with others, they impart the culture. *That's* leadership.

THE SELF-IDENTITY ISSUE

The third issue we faced was how we could help people self-identify as a leader. I think everyone is called to be a leader at some point. I don't believe every person is called to be the president of the United Sates or the lead pastor of a church or the CEO of a corporation. But everyone is called to influence the lives of others, and that is leadership. Everyone is called to serve, and that is leadership. Everyone has a calling from God, and when they begin to use their gifts and talents, as we read about in Ephesians 4, that is leadership. The problem is that most people don't self-identify as a leader. Instead, they think the leader is someone else, usually the person with a title.

Our problem was we didn't want to simply tell everyone, "Hey, you're a leader!" We wanted to help them develop into that reality as we walked with them on their journey. Building people *is* the job, right? And that means walking with people, working with people as they develop at their own God-ordained pace.

So how do you ease people into that simple understanding that they are leaders without scaring them or creating in them a false expectation that they are ready to manage more than they are truly capable of handling at this stage of development? The answer came with the ousting of the volunteer vocabulary and the adoption of the SERVE model.

We lumped all of our ministry teams and roles under the banner of the SERVE team—worship teams, small group leaders, parking lot teams, outreach teams, everyone. Next we printed and distributed Manna SERVE T-shirts to those who serve in weekend services, with the exception of the worship team (they wear cool clothes). At first glance, it looks like the T-shirt is simply saying what the person appears to be doing: serving.

By the time people reach the third component of our pipeline or growth track (don't jump ahead!), they are introduced to SERVE as our definition of leadership, and suddenly they become aware that they have been functioning to some degree in the role of a developing leader all along.

MOVING PEOPLE FROM SERVING TO LEADING

The fourth issue we faced was how to funnel people who were meeting the service needs of the church into intentional leadership development training. And that's the whole purpose of this book. This is where a leadership-development culture, shoulder tapping, and a leadership-development pipeline converge.

We had to address an age-old question: Are leaders born or are they built? Of course, everyone knows the answer. Yes. Yes to both. Yet the truth is, even natural-born leaders need building to maximize their inherent gifts. I think everyone has leadership potential. Every mom is a leader. Every person with a testimony or a story is a leader, if you believe his or her story comes with a responsibility to share it. Even a twelve-year-old is in some way the leader of his eight-year-old brother or sister.

Further, I believe leadership potential goes well beyond the call to volunteer to fill a spot at church. As we established earlier in the book, the church exists to help people develop their callings (to the end that their world is changed), and that requires intentionality and systems. The intentionality has to do with a philosophy of leadership development, and the systems are shoulder tapping and a pipeline. These are the topics of the remaining chapters.

THE FOUNDATION
OF A LEADERSHIP-
DEVELOPMENT CULTURE

In chapter 2, we discussed the type of church that can be home to a true leadership-development culture. In this chapter, we will discuss the type of philosophical foundation that undergirds it. Words give expression to ideas, ideas frame language, and language defines culture. In this chapter, we'll outline six foundational ideas, philosophical pillars if you will, that are vital to a leadership-development culture.

1. THE ROLE OF THE CHURCH IS TO CREATE AN ENVIRONMENT WHERE GOD'S PEOPLE CAN DISCOVER AND MATURE IN THEIR CALLING SO THEY ARE EQUIPPED TO CHANGE THEIR WORLD.

Of course, everyone would agree with the proposition the church is here to change the world. But I'm not talking about changing *the* world; I want everyone to change *their* world. There's a huge difference. If the organization of the church sets out to change the world, it may accomplish the goal collectively, but in the process it's possible for the people to remain undeveloped in their individual callings. But if you equip and empower people to change *their* individual portion of the world, you build a disciple who is "thoroughly equipped for every good work," as Paul told Timothy in 2 Timothy 3:17. In the former, the world is impacted, but the believers remain weak. In the latter, you get both: the believers are being developed and the world is being impacted.

Don't get me wrong: I'm not against corporate outreach projects. Far from it, we do a ton of those every year. We have to in order to survive with the turnover rate in our city. I don't see this as an either-or proposition; I see this as a both-and proposition. I just think it's far easier to sign people up for corporate forays into the community on weekends than it is to mentor them for ministry on weekdays. I believe God has called every believer to change *their* world. The Great

Commission is not strictly a corporate mandate; it's an individual mandate as well.

How does a person discern the borders of her world? I think each person is responsible before God for her jurisdiction defined by her "bed, buck, and burden." Let me explain.

In Paul's sermon at Athens, he told the hearers: "From one man he [God] made all the nations, that they should inhabit the whole earth; and he marked out their appointed times in history and the boundaries of their lands" (Acts 17:26). My purpose here is not to debate theology concerning sovereignty and responsibility, but I think it's clear in Scripture that God placed us all here in a way that suits His purposes. I believe that extends to the place where we live, even to the exact dwelling. I know you chose your house or apartment, but you hoped and prayed that God would help you. Suppose He answered your prayer, and now there you are, in the dwelling of God's and your choosing. Bottom line: I think your bed—where you live—is part of your spiritual jurisdiction, and God has called you to make a difference there, in your city, in your neighborhood, and on your street.

Ever since the fall, we have had to labor to make the ground yield its fruit. We have had to work to make a living. And the biblical teaching on work is that work is good and good for us. I think our "buck"—where we earn our living—is part of our spiritual jurisdiction. It includes all the people in our work orbit. Some people might work in a specific space and deal with a specific group of people. A third-grade teacher's orbit, for example, would include some specific people: principals, administrators, other teachers, students, and parents. A Realtor's orbit is far less definable since the whole world is a potential client. What about students or people who don't have a job? The job of students at every educational level is to eventually get a job or create an income, so their spiritual jurisdiction includes the relationships generated through their schooling. People who are retired or without a job should see the people they routinely interface with as part of their orbit. Bottom line: the people we interact with in the course of our daily activities are part of our spiritual jurisdiction, and God has called us to impact them through our words, our actions, and our character.

Virtually everyone is burdened for something. By burdened, I mean there's something in life that interests them, something they're passionate about, something that makes them angry or makes them cry. For some people, that's human trafficking or literacy issues or racial equality. For others, it may be something at the other end of the spectrum, like gardening or sports. Whatever it is that our heart leans toward, God can use that burden to insert us into the orbits of others and use us in that place to impact their lives. When believers follow their heart and join a fantasy football league with the guys at the gym, they are putting themselves in a place where they can make a difference in the lives of the other guys in the league. Of course, if the burden falls into a social justice or human rights category, believers who join those circles can make an impact in the lives of the individuals with whom they interact as well as making this world a better place to live.

A church that begins with the philosophical proposition that all believers were made to count and to change *their* world, and the role of the church is to help them figure out how to do that, has the right mind-set to build a true leadership-development culture. It all begins with the notion that to fulfill the Great Commission, we're going to have to build these people!

2. BELIEVE MORE FOR OTHERS THAN THEY BELIEVE FOR THEMSELVES.

I've heard that love is the greatest change agent in the world, but I don't think that's true. I believe *faith* is the greatest agent of change, because the highest form of love—unconditional love—is in no way earned or deserved. People say this is the kind of love God shows to us, the kind of love we experienced when we first met Him and the kind of love He has exercised toward us ever since. In making this argument, they make my case for the power of love.

The kind of love we're talking about is the kind of love

that accepts us as we are. It seems as though almost every Billy Graham Crusade I saw while I was growing up ended with the hymn "Just as I Am," the first two lines of which are "Just as I am, without one plea, but that thy blood was shed for me." Love says, "Come to me just as you are—broken, sinful, condemned—and I will accept you!" Love shows mercy and takes us in. It makes outsiders part of the family. It forgives and extends compassion even where it isn't (especially where it isn't) deserved. Love is vital, and if it weren't for love, we would all be lost. I am not belittling love. I just don't think love is the greatest change agent in the world. But faith is.

Faith begins with love. I accept you as you are and where you are. But then faith elevates you to a different place. Faith says, "You may be a mess today, but I see a better tomorrow for you!" Faith is always future, always looking forward, never satisfied with the status quo. Faith's posture is always, "There is more. Your best days are yet ahead."

Faith is more than mere optimism. Optimism is a wish, a hope. Faith has the capacity to open your eyes to a newer, better version of you. Faith has the ability to make you believe in things you can't yet see. Hebrews 11:1 puts it this way: "Now faith is confidence in what we hope for and assurance about what we do not see." Loves accepts you, but faith pulls you up to another level, and that's why faith is the greatest change agent in the world.

It's one thing to have faith in God for salvation, but it's

quite another to have faith in God for yourself. When we come to Him, His Spirit convicts us that we are sinners in need of a Savior. Then He points us to Jesus. Talk about amazing grace! Then He bids us to walk with Him while He transforms us. It is so easy to get transfixed on our obvious sinfulness. I say obvious because the closer we get to Him, the more sinful we appear. As we draw near, His light reveals what we always feared to be true: we are more lost than we knew. On the flip side, our grasp of grace grows stronger, and thanksgiving flows more readily from our lips. Now we get it; we were and are sinners in need of a Savior.

But God says: *"I can make you different. I can change you. The same grace that redeemed you can rebuild you."*

And we say, "Amen." But in truth, it is often easier to believe that for others than it is to believe it about ourselves. And if it weren't enough that we often have a hard time with that concept for ourselves, the people around us and the enemy of our souls have plenty to say to underscore our sinful ineptitude. Enter another key philosophical pillar of a leadership-development culture.

In a world filled with negativity, folks are desperate to find a place where people believe more for them than they do for themselves. When faith for others' lives reaches a tipping point in a church, when a driving force in the hearts of the leadership is believing more for others than they do for themselves, that place begins to come alive with an almost irresistible magnetism. People want to believe God has better things in life for them, but they dare not step out lest they be disappointed. Instead, they wait and wonder, *Does anyone really think God has a place of significance for me?*

How powerful is it to open your arms and say, "Just look around, my friend; there are some powerful and amazing stories all over this place"? You would be amazed to hear the stories from the lives of the SERVE team members who are leading you, serving you right now. God's calling on your life and His plan for you will blow your mind!" A church that has this reality as part of its philosophical mind-set is forming the basis for a leadership-development culture.

3. BUILD THE MAJORITY OF YOUR LEADERS WITHIN THE HOUSE.

We have established the idea that everything we need to reach our city is already in the house, which leads us to this next foundational idea of a leadership-development culture. We discussed in previous chapters the fact that most churches buy their top leaders from other churches rather than build them inside the house. And I've shared that we write about 120 paychecks, and of those 120 leaders, 113 were built inside the house. Three of the four leaders on our lead team began as janitors. They were built inside the house. So what does *build* mean? Is that the leadership-development pipeline? No, the pipeline is a system, and having a simple, clear system is vital. Building is far more organic, but it always includes a three-step process: discover, develop, deploy.

I'll never forget when our firstborn discovered his toes. He was absolutely amazed. He stared at them, grabbed them, tugged on them, chewed on them. He had no idea they had been there the entire time. I guess that's why we call it discovery.

If you think about it, every stage begins with discovery: a new idea, an uncovering of what was always there but somehow not obvious, a breakthrough in character or capability. Learning is at the core of discovery. All through life, from infancy to maturity, discovery is the beginning of something new. So building people, at every level and at every new phase, always begins with a discovery. Perhaps they discover something about their calling or a spiritual gift they didn't know they had. Perhaps they discover a burden or become convicted that they need to learn to become effective in sharing their faith. Perhaps they finally learn, after years of being told by seemingly everybody, they are hardheaded and stubborn. Perhaps they come to the realization they cannot overcome this sin on their own.

Sometimes discovery is a revelation, as in God shows us something. At other times discovery can result from a discus-. sion with a leader or a friend. "I think you'd be really good at . . ." Or maybe it's a tougher conversation: "I really don't think you're very good at . . ." After all, sometimes it's just as important to know who we aren't as it is to know who we are. In fact, often we really can't know who we are until we have discovered who we aren't. Sometimes discovery comes from experimentation and trial and error. Perhaps they try to lead a small group on a particular topic, or they try their hand at teaching others, or students step out to share their faith with a friend.

Reaching back to chapter 2, this is why the church must be a grace-filled environment where failure is not fatal. If people aren't free to try and fail and try again, then the atmosphere of discovery is short-circuited. In that case, only the boldest will try something new. If you want members to grow, and if discovery is always the first step, then people have to feel safe to fail.

The next step in the process is development. This can mean a whole range of things, but it is always in response to a discovery. A person who has discovered he is the problem in his marriage might need marriage counseling or a mentor. Someone who has discovered an aptitude in a certain area may require formal education. A person who has discovered a new job opportunity might need training. Depending on the discovery, development in that area could mean a wide variety of things. Some could be short-term: attend a class, make a budget, join a small group or a SERVE team, ask forgiveness, learn how to journal. The list is endless. Long-term development might include learning to control your temper, living free from lust, growing in your capacity to counsel or lead, building a great marriage, and so forth.

But here is the really cool part: *almost all the resources necessary for people to develop are already in the house.* Friends, prayer, guidance, small groups, mentoring, spiritual parents, entrepreneurs, counselors (formal and informal), and business leaders are all part of the body. Over the years, for example, I have seen building contractors and business leaders from other fields elevate an employee who was discovered to have a particular talent to a place of leadership, often culminating in that employee opening their own company. The funny thing to me is that the people often involved in mentoring the individual never would have classified what they were doing as spiritual, since the field in which they were training them was allegedly secular. But helping someone develop in any area of life is a keen spiritual exercise!

I have seen people from broken homes learn about family by being attached to spiritual, almost surrogate parents. I personally have learned some very helpful things about finances while riding with a businessman on bike rides with a triathlon small group. I have seen SERVE team leaders take potential leaders under their wing to train and empower them to lead. The truth is, everyone can have a hand in developing others, and when people get the idea that this is normal, this is how the Christian life was meant to work, you begin to find yourself in the midst of a self-feeding leadership-development culture. Again, the pipeline is the system, but developing people is the second part of the messy, life-upon-life process of discipleship.

In a military context, deploy means to be sent into action. I like that definition. Sometimes a deployment is a big event with fanfare, such as when an entire unit deploys. But often it is the natural flow of military life: one goes out and another comes back. Either way, deployment is part and parcel of being in the military. The army is constantly training, and all its training is to prepare its people to deploy.

I love the obvious connection to church life. In the context of the local church, training equals development and development leads to one of three camps. We can develop in our *character*, our *competency*, and our *chemistry*. In other words, we grow personally into greater Christlikeness. We grow in our ministry and leadership abilities. We grow in our ability to get along with others and live out the values of our culture. And like the army, all training, all development, all growth has a purpose: to deploy. In the church this means that God does not lead us into the development phase simply for our own sake. He is developing us to use us in the lives of others. That's why everyone is a leader at some level. God loves to take our tragedies to bring us to triumph and to build a testimony of His grace.

To deploy simply means to use what God has done in

our lives to help others. When people catch this, when they make this the foundation of the small-group system, when they routinely hear from the pulpit that tragedy, triumph, and testimony are part of God's plan from the beginning, and (most importantly) when they begin to do it, then your leadership-development culture has begun to hit the all-by-itself stage. The culture replenishes itself. It operates on its own. It becomes like a living thing.

This process—discovering, developing, deploying—never ends. It is how people, ranging from new believers to seasoned saints, grow to become who God has called them to become. If you think about it, every milestone in your life began with a discovery. Then you developed in that area until you stepped into it (deployed) as your own.

4. VALUE CHARACTER OVER ANOINTING AND GIFTING. ANOINTING CAN COME IN A MICROWAVE, BUT CHARACTER GROWS IN A CROCK-POT.

In a troubled economy, credit is costly, markets are volatile, and cash is king. The idea is that cash is more valuable than any other investment tool. Cash is the most stable, most valuable commodity in hard times. In the kingdom of God (and in all of life), character is king. It is the currency of the kingdom.

If it's true that God is interested in conforming us to Christlikeness, and if it is true that building people *is* the job, then it is obvious that our focus should be on character. Being quick to repent, becoming self-aware, living generously, exhibiting kindness under pressure, developing self-control in areas of former weakness or sin, learning to listen instead of talk, treating people with respect (especially people who grate on us), being quick to forgive, learning how to be a peacemaker, and developing courage (to list a few things) are things that truly make one a leader.

These things give a person real authority. In the kingdom and in life, authority does not come from a position. It comes from your life. It flows from who you have become. We can all name people we've worked for who had a position of authority but had no real authority in their lives. We were forced to do what they said because they were our boss, but we never truly respected them. Given a choice, we never would have followed them, but we were required to. In contrast, there are people we gravitate toward because they seem to have a special quality that sets them apart. They live life from the inside out. They seem to draw on an inner strength, an inner grace. They are centered people. They seem to know who they are as well as who they aren't, and they are comfortable with that. They have a quiet confidence, a strength of soul. When we think of them, words like *integrity, trustworthy, dependable,* and *generous* come to mind. They have authority, but I'm not taking about a personality type but rather something that informs all personality types. I'm talking about character.

Jesus and the religious leaders of His day are a perfect illustration of this point. The scribes and Pharisees of the first century were people of position, and because of that they had power. They occupied roles that allowed them to establish the spiritual climate and set the religious agenda of the nation. They were in positions of authority. Jesus, on the other hand, had no official position in Israel. He was called rabbi, which means teacher, only because He had a following. His authority came from who He was as a person. Remember, the vast majority of people had no idea He was the second person of the Trinity, but they could tell He had authority.

> The people were amazed at his teaching, because he taught them as one who had authority, not as the teachers of the law. (Mark 1:22)

> They were amazed at his teaching, because his words had authority. (Luke 4:32)

Jesus was the ultimate person of character, the gold standard, and it showed in His life and every time He opened His mouth to speak.

Now I'm not against people being in positions of authority. I have occupied positions of authority nearly my whole life. And I'm not advocating the removal of roles to which some measure of authority is attached. For any organization and for all of society to function in an orderly fashion, roles and layers of positional authority are required. My point is that real authority, truly being a leader, is derived from who you are and who you have become, not what you do. Remember, if no one is following, you may have a position, but you aren't a leader.

If character is king, and our focus should be on the virtues that make for character, then why do we so easily gravitate toward people who are gifted or skilled or talented? While we may say that character is the most important thing, our internal promotion and recruitment practices, as well as our hiring practices, often say a different thing. We tend to focus more on doing than on being.

When I say choose character over anointing or gifting or skill, I am not saying we should despise skill. I'm saying we should prioritize character. Everyone has a character cap, and the gap between your calling and your character is the danger zone. The apostle Paul made the same case in Ephesians 4:1–3: "As a prisoner for the Lord, then, I urge you to live a life worthy of the calling you have received. Be completely humble and gentle; be patient, bearing with one another in love. Make every effort to keep the unity of the Spirit through the bond of peace." He stated the proposition that every believer has a calling and that we should live a life worthy of it. And how is that done? The instruction that follows is all about character.

We've all likely been burned by a leader whose character hadn't caught up to his calling and gifting. Sadly, some leader or organization, enamored with his talent, gifts, or natural skill, pushed the person forward before he was ready. The result is often a shipwreck and people are hurt. Kindness and wisdom would dictate that we hold a high-talent, less-character person back until his character begins to bridge the gap. In fact, that process itself produces an opportunity for character to be developed.

I'm not saying we should choose character as opposed to skill or talent. That would be foolish and unbiblical. Paul's letters to Timothy and Titus were all about helping these leaders further develop and enhance their ministry skill. Ideally, you want a person to develop in both character and skill, but the former is harder to develop than the latter. I often tell the people I am mentoring: "I am much more interested in your character than your talent. I can teach you all sorts of skills, but character is a slow and painful build. Talent can get you there, but only character can keep you there."

Leadership is, in fact, a combination of both character *and* skill. Both are needed in leaders to help grow the local church and move the kingdom of God forward. In his talk to the Rapid Growth Learning Community at Leadership Network,

Mark Miller likened the combination of character and skill in leadership to an iceberg. As you know, a huge portion of an iceberg is underwater and unseen to the naked eye. Leadership is like that too. In Mark's view, character, the unseen portion, is about 70 percent of leadership, and the more obvious skills comprise the other 30 percent. Both are required, but the scale must tip in favor of character. If you develop people who are all skills but weak in character, they will help build the local church, but they will likely build it in the direction of their own vision, and that could be dangerous. That being said, if you develop people who are all character and no skills, they'll be safe, but they won't build anything.[1] In David, we see a leader who possessed both: "David shepherded them with integrity of heart; with skillful hands he led them" (Ps. 78:72).

Building people is about who they become—not just what they can do. Keeping our eye on the main thing—character, the currency of the kingdom—is paramount in developing a leadership-development culture.

5. DON'T BUILD PEOPLE TO BUILD THE HOUSE. BUILD PEOPLE AND THE RESULT WILL BE THAT THE HOUSE GETS BUILT.

This is an issue of motive. It brings us to the why question. Why do we want to build more leaders? Why do we want to create a leadership-development pipeline? If the goal is to simply build a bigger church, as in higher attendance, then we have missed the mark. But I am certainly not saying that it is a bad idea to work hard at growing a local church. Our church is large, and we intend for it to get larger. But building a large church is not the goal. Building people is the goal, and when we build people, the church will grow as a result. Go back to Ephesians 4:11–16 and look at the progression. Those in vocational ministry equip the people, and the people do the work of the ministry. As the members of the body do their part in the way God prescribed it, the church builds itself up in quality (character) and quantity (continued growth). It all goes back to building people and building leaders. (It's well-documented that successfully growing a local church is a much more sophisticated process than simply adding some more leaders. But it is also true that a church cannot sustain growth without an increasing supply of leaders.)

It sounds like I am arguing semantics and that both ideas are somehow the same. But they are not. The one says, "We'll be stuck here unless we develop some more leaders so the church can grow." The other says, "Let's develop people into their callings. And look, the church is growing."

Drilling down a little more on the motive issue, we need to honestly ask ourselves, are we truly building people for the sake of the people so they can become all that God is calling them to be, or are we using this idea as a method to draw people into local church volunteerism so we can fulfill our own calling and vision? I am not the judge, and only the Holy Spirit can reveal the true motives of our hearts, but in terms of full disclosure, I admit I have found myself in that trap more than once. It sounds subtle but it's really not. It boils down to the following questions: Am I building people for their sake or my sake? Am I building them to empower them or use them? Am I building them for His glory or my own?

Since the beginning of time, leaders have been using people to accomplish their own goals. But Jesus told the disciples the church was to operate under a different motivation.

> Jesus called them together and said, "You know that the rulers of the Gentiles lord it over them, and their high officials exercise authority over them. Not so with you. Instead, whoever wants to become great among you must be your servant, and whoever wants to be first must be your slave—just as the Son of Man did not come to be served, but to serve, and to give his life as a ransom for many." (Matt. 20:25–28)

In effect, Jesus was saying, "Leaders serve people for the good of the people, just like I am serving you by laying down My life for you."

Why is this motivation question so important? Because what is truly in your heart will come out in so many subtle but powerful ways—through what you say and how you say it, what you count and what makes you cry, what you celebrate and what you correct. Your true heart comes through in your tone and body language. At the end of the day, you can try to fake it, but what's in your heart will find a way to express itself to others. And that subtle communication makes a much greater impact on the lives of those around you than the words you speak.

We have all had teachers, coaches, bosses, even parents whose words gave approval but their nonverbals communicated disapproval. We've been around people whose words said kindness but their demeanor conveyed contempt. We tend to put much more stock in what we pick up from people through nonverbal communication than we do through the actual words they say. People aren't stupid. They know when they are being used to build someone else's dream. They can tell the difference when someone says, "We are here to help you grow in your walk with God," but the heart says, "I need you to volunteer to do these jobs so this church can grow and fulfill my vision, make my dream come true."

The heart will express itself in a multitude of ways, some obvious and some subtle. But make no mistake: the true disposition of the heart cannot be hidden. When the hearts of the leaders in a church truly believe their mission is to help people discover, develop, and deploy into their calling to the end that their world is being changed, when they believe more for others than people do for themselves, that passion will reveal itself. It cannot be hidden, and it's that heart, from a philosophical perspective, that helps drive a leadership-development culture.

6. GET THE SERVE EQUATION RIGHT!

In chapter 4, I made the case for the SERVE model of leadership, and it's clear in the Gospels that Jesus viewed leadership through the lens of servanthood. So in our twenty-first century context, what does the serve equation look like? Is the one serving greater than the one being served? Or is the one being served greater than the one serving? In our society, the latter is the equation in use. When you sit down in a restaurant, the one being served (the customer) is clearly viewed as greater than the one serving (the wait staff). In contemporary culture, people who fill the role of servants are "less." People who occupy the authority role are viewed as "greater." Wherever we go—get on a bus, walk into a furniture store, go to an amusement park—the equation holds true. Those serving are viewed as less, and those being served are viewed as greater.

Jesus would have a problem with that. Let's look at Luke's parallel to Matthew 20:25–28:

A dispute arose among them as to which of them was considered to be greatest. Jesus said to them, "The kings of the

Gentiles lord it over them; and those who exercise authority over them call themselves Benefactors. But you are not to be like that. Instead, the greatest among you should be like the youngest, and the one who rules like the one who serves. For who is greater, the one who is at the table or the one who serves? Is it not the one who is at the table? But I am among you as one who serves." (Luke 22:24–27)

In this passage Jesus acknowledges that society looks at the servant as the lesser player in human interactions, but then He adds a penetrating last line: "But I am among you as one who serves." He claims the role of "one who serves"! No one is greater than Jesus, and He has chosen the posture of a servant. The problem was, the disciples wanted to be on top; they wanted to be great. And Jesus never rebuked them for that. Instead, He showed them how to get there.

In both Matthew 20:25–28 and Luke 22:24–27, Jesus makes it clear that the church (as an organization) and believers (as individuals) should view leadership and servanthood differently than the world does. The goal is the same—to be great—but the methods to achieve that goal are polar opposites. It all goes back to how one views people.

So, what equation should we use as believers and as leaders in the church? Is it, "I'm great, so you serve me"? (While this equation is in use in many quarters, it is so obviously arrogant that no one would admit to it.) Or is it, "I'm great, so

I serve you"? (This is so condescending and so *not* the demeanor of Jesus.) Or could it be, "I become great when I make you great"? (I think this captures the spirit of the text.)

In my view, becoming great means using the leadership God has given you to do great things for Him in advancing His kingdom on earth—building an army of disciples who carry His passions, live out His values, and become His hands and feet, boldly doing His will. A leadership-development culture is undercut by the "serve me and my vision" mentality, but it is enhanced and empowered by the "I serve you and make you great" mentality. Get the serve equation right.

SHOULDER TAPPING AND
THE WAY TEAMS ARE BUILT

I have been privileged to serve for a number of years as a mentor for a group of some of Europe's most influential pastors. At one of our gatherings I was asked to speak on leadership development. During the robust question-and-answer session that followed, one of the leaders asked, "What one thing is crucial—must every church do—in order to shift a church from a volunteer culture to a leadership-development culture?" Without hesitation, I answered, "Shoulder tapping!"

Earlier in the book, I bordered on boasting about the fact that we have a lot of leaders. My heart is not to boast, but let me be honest. We have a huge turnover rate because of the military community in which we serve, and on top of that, due to the nature of how the Department of Defense works, we cannot predict who will go when. We're flying blind in terms of future planning. And yet we are engaged in a multiply strategy and are actively, aggressively sending people out to plant churches near every US military base in the world. Lots of people are going out the door, either because Uncle Sam is taking them or because we are sending them ourselves. In the midst of this activity we have compiled lists of leaders—leaders who are ready to plant, leaders we are developing to plant, leaders who are ready to join a staff, leaders we are developing to join a staff, leaders who are ready to step up to top SERVE team roles, and leaders we are developing for those roles.

In fact, we have scheduled a lead team retreat to work through four lists of leaders at four levels of development. We will move some from one list to another based on their growth (the upward draft), thus making room for others. We will add new people to the lists and discuss who is next to plant or fill other ministry roles. I can't wait. I love this! Everywhere I look, I see new leaders stepping up, young leaders setting their sights on lofty God-ordained goals, leaders taking other leaders under their wing, preparing them for their future. This is like working in a leadership factory, and I wake up every day thinking about how to make it better.

But when I think back over the thirty years we have been building in this way and ask myself, "When did this really take off?" I clearly know the answer. It took off when I drew a line in the sand and made shoulder tapping the law of the land.

What does shoulder tapping mean? As I said earlier, when we invite people into ministry, ask them to join a team or serve in any capacity, we *do not* pass out clipboards.

> We *do not* preach sermons on how great it is to work in the children's ministry.
>
> We *do not* have a connection center (which we all know is really a volunteer-booth masquerading as a way to get connected).
>
> We *do not* pass out invitation cards to join a ministry.
>
> We *do not* have a commitment Sunday or preach a commitment series.
>
> We *do not* have fancy little response cards taped under the seats.
>
> We *do not* have a ministry fair to get people to join ministry teams.
>
> We *do not* have a sign-up sheet beside each classroom door to recruit helpers.
>
> Bottom line, we *do not* use mass appeals of any type. It is amazing all the things people have come up with to get other people to volunteer! We *do not* do those things.

We shoulder tap. Period.

There are two caveats. First, we have three "My Manna

Connection Nights" (MMCN) where people at every site get a chance to interact firsthand with our small groups. We are a small-group church, and everything at our church is a small group. We use a free-market small-group system, which means there are all kinds of groups, all of which are described in an online catalog. But it helps people to see a display and talk to the leaders face-to-face. Most people sign up online, and the majority of people who come to an MMCN are new and seeking to find a small-group connection. However, we *never* do any type of recruitment for leaders at an MMCN, nor do we ask people to sign up to join any teams. MMCN is only to help people find a small group.

Second, we give people a chance to sign up for one-time outreaches. These are not ongoing ministries, and we are not building SERVE teams with these outreaches. The only way we recruit SERVE team members (parking lot, small-group leaders, greeters, ushers, worship team, site hosts, security team, bus drivers, etc.) is through shoulder tapping.

Leadership is about producing *followership* because leaders first make followers (before they make other leaders). If you are leading but have no followers, then you are holding a position. You aren't leading. How then are leaders to attract followers into their ministry lane?

People are attracted to a leader's ministry lane in two ways: (1) they are drawn into ministry or (2) they are invited into ministry. People can be drawn into ministry by the charisma, vision, or character of leaders (their gifting and use of that gift). In other words, some people buy into leaders, and that's a good thing. People can also be invited into ministry. In the vast majority of churches, that invitation comes through some sort of mass appeal such as I described at the beginning of this chapter, and they are largely ineffective for the reasons I will enumerate later in this chapter. The most effective way to bring people into ministry and a key step in leadership development is shoulder tapping.

SHOULDER TAPPING INCLUDES FOUR KEY COMPONENTS

Shoulder tapping is an organic process and very fluid. It can take place in a passing conversation or it can be the result of a weeks-long process. It's both a skill and an art, but at the risk of making it appear like a four-part checklist, I am going to break it down into parts. It isn't a checklist, but I think shoulder tapping is better understood if we look at each segment separately and then demonstrate it in conversation form, which you'll find at the end of the chapter.

1. Selection: Who Are You Looking For?

Are you simply looking for volunteers, for doers? Doers are people who are happy to simply come every week and do the job you've asked them to do. Doers aren't bad people. Doers are people who have decided, at least at this time in their lives, they don't want to become a leader, even if they hold the position of leader. By becoming a leader, I mean to be developed (shaped, mentored) into a leader. Doers want to serve, but they don't want to or they don't know how to SERVE (as in the SERVE model outlined in chapter 4). The doer is the basic stock-in-trade volunteer: a person looking to belong and do some good for God along the way. I don't want to come across as unkind, but I am speaking in broad terms. To be fair, most doers are great people who see serving the church as part of serving God. But to be honest, most of them do not see their present role in service to the church as part of their development into the person God ultimately designed them to be. They're just serving.

Sadly, most church leaders today are more than happy to fill the roles of volunteer positions with whomever they can get. More often than not, they wind up with hundreds of doers (volunteers, not leaders). The idea is, "We'll put together a program and teach them to be leaders later. Right now, we just need workers to feed the machine." Bad idea. Here's why.

First, doers respond to need and leaders respond to vision. Every form of mass appeal is designed to motivate people to respond to serve from the vantage point of need:

- The church needs help.
- You need to learn to serve.

- We can't take the next step as a church unless we get help.
- You will grow if you'll serve.
- We have the best children's ministry in the city, but it can be better with your help.

The vast majority of people who fill out the cards, sign up at the desk, or answer the call in some other way are doers (people willing to volunteer to meet a need).

Leaders, on the other hand, respond to vision. It is, in fact, that visioning capacity that makes them leaders. Most natural leaders are looking to make a difference, not fill a spot, and so they aren't often attracted by mass appeals.

We've all been there. You preached your best "let's get committed" series and 450 people signed up on the cards provided at their seats. You think to yourself, *Boy, this is going to be a volunteer harvest!* And even though only 275 of them turn up for the Sunday afternoon volunteer orientation meeting or one-hour training session, you're still pretty excited. So you divide them into the four or five ministry lanes and send them off for training.

But as you look around the room, although you'd never admit it, you'd be happy for some of these people to go home. Some of them are just not the people you were hoping for. On top of that, you wonder to yourself, *Where are the Jenkinses, the Thompsons, and the Greens—the people with great families, great jobs, people of position and power, the obvious natural leaders? They love Jesus and seem to love the church. Why aren't they here?*

The answer is that they do love Jesus and they do love the church, but they are leaders, and leaders don't respond to need. *Leaders respond to vision.* But you decide to make the most of the situation, and off the people (mostly doers) go for training. Two months later, only a handful of the people who came to the orientation are still faithfully serving, and you wish some of those would unvolunteer. You wonder, *Do I just have bad people?*

No, you have great people: people with a magnificent calling from God. You just have a bad method.

The quintessential doer loves Jesus and the church and expresses that love through serving. They get involved in some ministry and give it their all. Faithfully, every week, they work, serving God and others—with their head *down*. By that I mean, their focus is on the work. Rarely do they look up, metaphorically speaking, to see what is happening elsewhere. Theirs is the lane that matters most. Children, greeting, outreach, worship, or small groups—this is where it is! Since their head is down—doing—they often don't notice the number of workers in their lane has dwindled, at least not until they begin to feel the pressure of producing more with less. They also begin to feel abandoned by the leadership. *Why won't they help us? Send us some volunteers? Surely they see how crucial our lane is! Someone needs to talk to them!* And that is how you determined you needed to preach another commitment series or have a volunteer Sunday or hold a ministry fair—to fill the ranks. Doers operate with their head down—doing.

What happens when you put a doer in a volunteer leadership position, say, in the parking lot, as a greeter, or in the children's ministry? The leadership-development process ends right there. Why? Because doers do, they *do* ministry; they don't *lead* ministry. And people attract other people who are like themselves. So doers attract other doers, not leaders.

In his book *21 Irrefutable Laws of Leadership,* John Maxwell describes the "law of the lid."[1] It's a simple but profound idea. Everyone has a leadership quotient on a scale of one to ten. Leaders can attract and lead other leaders who are on the same level or lower, but not those with a higher quotient. So a six can attract and lead other sixes and below, but a seven or an eight will not stick around for long. A person can move up the ladder from a four to a five or from a six to a seven by growing and being developed as a leader. And a true leadership-development culture is focused on making that happen—helping everyone grow in their leadership capacity.[2]

Sadly, a volunteer-driven culture is focused on getting people to volunteer so the "machine" can operate properly. Often, leadership development is neglected or perhaps relegated to a class. When you promote a doer to the leadership level in ministry, you dumb down the leadership potential in that ministry. As a result, that ministry gets weaker, and its effectiveness wanes. First, the people attracted to a ministry led by a doer are more than likely doers themselves. A three will not attract and keep a six. Second, the development of the leadership potential in others who join the ministry often grinds to a halt.

Remember what leaders do: they SERVE (chapter 4). They **see** the future. A seven sees the future more clearly than a three. They see how the ministry they lead fits into the vision of the church. There is that word—*vision*—which is the key to attracting other leaders. Leaders lead with their heads up, not down. They see the future, not just the work being done.

A seven will **engage** and develop others better than a three. In fact, a three may not engage many people at all. They will likely depend on church leadership to engage people for them using mass appeals. And a three cannot develop anyone beyond their own level. Soon the whole ministry is in danger of being capped at level three. If the leader is a three, the whole ministry reaches its lid at three.

Leaders **reinvent** continually, and that's very hard to do when your head is down, serving, and you can't clearly see how this ministry fits into the overall vision of the church.

Leaders **value** relationships and results. They understand a win and how the ministry they lead contributes to that win. Doers focus on the job at hand, heads down.

Leaders **embody** the values, but doers concentrate on their lane: outreach, ushering, their small group.

If your target is warm bodies to fill ministry roles, you can find them through mass appeals, but you can never build a leadership culture that way. If you want to grow people, along with getting ministry done, you'll need to promote leaders. That is how leadership development becomes a culture. That is how the development of others becomes self-perpetuating. That process begins when we select the right people—leaders. And that happens through shoulder tapping.

People will do what was done to them. If they were mentored, they will most likely mentor others. If they were shoulder tapped, they will most likely shoulder tap others, especially if the preponderance of those serving alongside them were also shoulder tapped. If they were trained and acculturated in a leadership-development pipeline, they will send (recruit) others like themselves to attend as well.

When you promote leaders into leadership in unpaid volunteer positions, especially if the leaders were built inside the house, you organically perpetuate the process whereby leaders beget leaders, metaphorically speaking. When fours and fives join a ministry led by a seven who has developed some fours into fives and some fives into sixes, there is an automatic upward draft. People who find themselves in that ministry orbit begin to develop an awareness that they, too, have a calling and find themselves believing they truly can become the people God designed them to be.

Doers are driven by service; leaders are driven by vision. Therefore, the people who lead a ministry *must* be leaders who are growing and developing themselves and who know how to grow and develop others. If the plan is to always promote from within the ministry lane (and in the case of paid vocational ministry leaders and pastors, from within the church), then there must be a plethora of growing leaders in each lane. That doesn't happen by accident. That only happens on purpose. That happens because the people in the lane were shoulder tapped—hand-selected.

I have heard that eagles (leaders) don't flock. It may be true that literal eagles don't flock, but leaders do *if* they are surrounded by other people who lead with vision, people who SERVE.

> Leaders are attracted to people who *see* the future, who understand the vision and can relate to others how the ministry they lead is vital to the accomplishment of that vision.
>
> Leaders want to be around people who will *engage* and develop them in their calling. Above all else, leaders want to know they count.
>
> Leaders gravitate toward other leaders who let them share in the process of building the ministry, and

that's what happens when a leader is willing to
reinvent continually.

Leaders want to win and enjoy the win with others,
which is what happens when the one in charge *values*
results and relationships.

Leaders are attracted to other leaders who are genuine
and *embody* the values.

Jennifer is a thirty-two-year-old mother of three who was married right out of high school. She loves Jesus and her family. In fact, she feels her calling is to be a mom. Her passion is to—with her husband, Peter—rear their children to be world changers. She loves her church and was more than happy to consider serving in the children's ministry; it seemed right down her alley. She was an easy mark: a young, committed mom of three kids.

But whoever invited her into ministry got more than they bargained for. Somewhere along the way, early in her involvement in serving in the elementary small groups, someone told Jennifer that more than 80 percent of people who come to Christ do so under the age of eighteen. She couldn't sleep that night, so she got up and went online to further research that idea. Sure enough, it was true. She couldn't stop thinking about it.

She reasoned: "Our church does *so* many outreaches to win people to Christ. We send *so* many people and *so* much money overseas to reach people there as well. But by far, the biggest harvest is among the young—kids who attend our church every week!"

By week's end, she cornered her husband: "How can you be satisfied helping people find seats in the auditorium and adjusting thermostats when right down the hall part of the world's greatest harvest is happening each weekend? You need to quit helping late-comers find seats and join me in this work!"

Within two weeks, Peter had quit the usher team and was serving in the elementary department. He clearly saw the mission, thanks to his wife. Before too long, three other couples from the small group Peter and Jennifer attend were also serving among the same group of kids. They, too, were drawn in by the magnetic pull of the vision that burned in Jennifer's heart.

Together they hatched the idea that more kids would come to Christ if they built a prayer team to undergird their work, so they recruited prayer team members with a heart for kids. Jennifer and her husband and friends know that it may not look like much to most people, but they are playing a valuable—a crucial—part in their church's mission to reach people in their city for Christ.

Jennifer never went to college and she is not overtly talented. She never worked on Wall Street or argued a case in court. She never built a house or ran a restaurant. She isn't in the top 25 percent of incomes and she has no aspirations to run for Congress. But she's a leader. She saw the future. She engaged and developed others. Together they reinvented the role and added a prayer team. She values her friendships and, with her teammates, delights each weekend to add the names of kids they see come to Christ to the list of those who are candidates for baptism. No one has to call her and remind her of her duties or work to keep her motivated. Jennifer embodies her values.

As the church grew, it was decided to add some staff to the children's ministry. The children's pastor didn't need to look far to find candidates. There were lots of great leaders being built inside the house: people with a vision who already had the church's culture, leaders who knew how to SERVE. Today, Jennifer is the elementary director, spreading her passion to dozens of other Jennifers.

The first and most important component of shoulder tapping is *selection*. Ask yourself, "Who am I looking for?" Who is your ideal small-group leader, outreach leader, usher, greeter, receptionist, youth director? Are you just looking for volunteers or are you looking for leaders?

2. Connection: You Invite Them In

Another reason I do not favor mass appeals is because responders select you; you don't select them. And there is no one more suited to determine who fits in the ministry you lead than you. Through mass appeals you end up filling positions with people who may not fit. And even if they do fit, the overall vision level in the ministry you lead may take a drastic dip until you can develop those people into higher levels of leadership. In the meantime, this situation inhibits your ability to recruit other leaders, since leaders respond to vision.

The connection component has three stages:

1. Talk to them: what you see in them
2. Talk about your vision: why you do what you do
3. Talk about the opportunity: how you think they fit

Of course, you can't see potential leaders unless you are a leader yourself. Remember, leaders lead with their heads up. They aren't doing ministry; they're leading ministry, that is, leading the people who are doing the ministry. The leader of the 11:00 a.m. greeting team at the Elm Street campus used to greet people, but now that she is the leader of the team, her focus is on her team and the future leaders she will recruit to join the team. She doesn't greet. She takes care of the team: empowering them, encouraging them, mentoring them, motivating them. And she is constantly looking for whom she will invite to join her team. Her head is up. And once she sees someone she thinks might be a candidate for her team, she seeks to make a connection.

There is no magic to this point and it's not complicated. This is all about having conversations. Since the shoulder tapper already has a profile in her mind of the type of person she wants to recruit, all she has to do is look for people who fit the profile. Since she is leading with her head up, she can see hundreds of potential candidates. All she has to do is be friendly and follow her gut. Maybe she is looking for people who are friendly, people who are nicely dressed, people who look others in the eye when they engage them, people who easily smile.

Once she spots a few of those, it's time to go to work. She introduces herself and begins to interact and ask questions. She's looking for chemistry. Would this person fit well with her team? She is looking for competence. Does this person have the kind of personality required to make others feel welcomed and at home in this church? She is looking for character, which may be more difficult to discern. That is why shoulder tapping is a skill as well as an art. The skill side can be learned, but the art side only comes through trial and error. (That is also part of growing as a leader.)

There may be several conversations over a period of weeks before she approaches a candidate. In fact, she will likely talk to a number of people who, over time, just don't seem like a good fit. And that's okay.

Once she thinks she has a few candidates, she begins to talk about what she sees in them that would make them a good team member. She will talk in general terms about the vision of the church and share how the lane she leads relates to that vision. She will talk about her team, who they are and how they operate together. Further, she will talk with the candidates about how they might fit in. At any point if the candidates seem uninterested, she simply drops the idea and moves on. Actually, she is constantly talking to people, constantly looking for the next team member, so she is not desperate. Therefore, passing on a person is not a failure; it's just part of the process. She's not just trying to fill a spot; she is looking for a new leader to develop and she is constantly aware that the people she has been talking to might fit better in another spot in another ministry.

3. Vision: Raise the Bar

Vision and leadership go together. Natural leaders have a visioning capacity. It's no wonder that the first action of a leader in the SERVE model is *seeing* the future. In order for the leadership quotient of the team to stay high, the vision that drives the team has to be front and center. If some people don't resonate with the vision, it doesn't mean that they are bad people or that there is something wrong with them. It might be an indication that they belong in a different spot, on a different team. Or it might mean that this simply isn't the time for them to be on this particular team. And that's fine.

But when it comes to adding people to the team, they have to see it or they can't lead it. And since the real goal of the team is not just to get ministry done but to build, to develop the people who are doing it, the capacity to one day become a leader in this ministry is crucial. Just remember, if you can't see it, you can't lead it. That means that the third component—vision—is extremely important.

This is where shoulder tappers reveal a prejudice toward their ministry. They see it. They get it. And they feel this might just be the most important ministry in the church. For example:

- Outreach Team: What could be more important than leading people to Jesus?
- Worship Team: People change when they come into the proximity of His presence!
- Greeting Team: People have to feel they belong before they will believe.
- Children's Ministry: 80 percent of people come to Christ under the age of eighteen.
- Small Groups: The Great Commission is to make disciples, and discipleship happens in the context of a small group.
- Youth Ministry: We are building the next generation of leaders.

The list is endless. In fact, every ministry team needs to know exactly how and why their ministry function is vital to the fulfillment of the vision of the local church. How does this ministry help fulfill that mission?

But don't oversell it. We aren't begging anyone to join us. In fact, we are doing just the opposite. Make every effort to be discriminatory and do not hide that. First, every leader should know exactly how many people the team needs to operate at top capacity. Second, leaders should always talk to more people than the team needs because they are always looking for more people to develop. Therefore, it is not disingenuous to say, "I'm talking to three people, but I only have two slots open on this team right now." If you want to make your team stronger, recruit and build better players.

Don't ever beg anyone to join your team. Remember, if they can't see it, they can't lead it. Make sure you convey the idea that not everyone can do this job, so we can't take just anyone. End the conversation with the idea that the team needs people who can be all in. If they can't be fully committed, perhaps it might be best to wait for another day. Ask the person to earnestly pray and ask God if this ministry and being on this team is His next step for them: "Don't answer right now. Take some time and pray about it."

4. The Ask: Is This God's Next Step for You?

As I said earlier, shoulder tapping is fluid and organic. And its application varies from situation to situation. Sometimes it's serendipitous and sometimes it's planned. There are times when this is all one conversation and times when it is a series of conversations over time. At some point, a leader has to ask the candidate, "Do you want to be on this team?" However and whenever it is done, the ask should include three parts.

1. First, clarify the commitment. Exactly what are you asking them to do? What are the expectations? How many times per week or hours per weekend will they be expected to serve? How much preparation will be required? Are there any extra meetings? Make sure you communicate exactly what you expect from the candidate moving forward.

2. Second, caution candidates that they should feel this is part of God's plan for them right now, at this stage of their journey. Make sure they pray about it and feel God wants them to do this. When times get tough, you don't want them feeling you roped them into doing this. Instead, you want them believing God called them to this, so they need to grow in grace to be able to carry the load.

3. Finally, call them to commitment and welcome them to the team. This sounds so formal and it almost never is, but I am big on clarifying expectations up front. I believe that a lack of clarity concerning expectations is at the root of a great deal of pain in relationships.

A HYPOTHETICAL VIEW

As an example, let's say I'm leading the greeting team at the Cliffdale site during the 11:00 a.m. Sunday service. I know

I need sixteen people to operate this team effectively on any given Sunday, but I also know that people have lives and stuff sometimes happens. They can't always make it to church. There are vacations, sicknesses, deployments, runaway dogs, car trouble, and so on. Because of that, I'd be more comfortable with twenty people on my team. No problem. My head is always up and I'm always on the lookout.

One Sunday a guy catches my eye for the third week. He seems happy. There is a pep in his step. He is well-dressed, and every time I see him, he is fifteen minutes early. (And everybody knows that Christian standard time is fifteen minutes *after* the announced start time of any service.)

So I engage him in conversation. At first, it's just general stuff. Then I get around to asking him why he is here so early. "Bob, does your wife work in the children's ministry or something?" He says, "Actually she does, but that's not why I'm early. I just feel like ten minutes early is five minutes late." (Music to my ears.)

Over the next couple of weeks I grow to feel Bob would be a great addition to our team, so I begin to explain what we do and tie that generically to the vision of the church: "just trying to reach people."

Bob seems interested, so one Sunday when he walks in, I put my arm around him, point through the lobby doors into the worship center, and ask, "Bob, what happens in this room every week?"

He replies, "Well, you know, worship, announcements, some videos, an offering, a sermon, and an altar call."

I reply, "Wrong, Bob. That's just the delivery system. What happens in this room is life change. People's lives change inside this room every week. Now, let me ask you, whose life is more likely to change—a person who can't find a parking space, who has no idea where the bathrooms and the children's space are, who can't find four seats together, who was never greeted, and who leaves without anyone saying a word to him? Or a person who is enthusiastically greeted in the parking lot, escorted into the building where he is shown the children's space and easily spots the bathrooms, seated in the worship center, and warmly greeted as he leaves? You tell me, Bob, which person is more likely to experience life change?"

Bob replies, "The latter. He is more likely to experience life change."

Leaning in, I say to him, "That's what we do. We set people up for life change. We place the ball on the tee. And every week, people's lives change inside this room. You are probably thinking, *Why is he telling me this?* Well, over these last few weeks as we have been getting to know each other, I have the distinct impression you would fit very nicely on our team. I've prayed as well, and I want to offer you an opportunity to join us. But don't answer me now. I need to know you feel this is God's next step for you. I need your wife to feel good about it as well. I don't just need a warm body; I'm looking for someone who is motivated and who is ready to grow in their walk with God. I'm looking for people who really want to make a difference. Is that you, Bob? Again, don't tell me now. Pray about it, and let me know next week. But I need to tell you one more thing. I have four spots, and I am talking to seven people. The first four who tell me they're in are in. Thanks."

These types of conversations happen every week at our church. Again, shoulder tapping is a skill and an art. It's a skill you can learn and an art you can develop.

7

TOWARD BUILDING AN EFFECTIVE LEADERSHIP-DEVELOPMENT PIPELINE

Probably every student taking a course in church growth knows that a church eventually reduces to the size of its infrastructure. The idea is driven by the reality that a church is more than attendance; there are internal structures and processes that make a church what it is: small groups, guest follow-up, prayer groups, worship teams, outreaches, weekend services, children's ministry, financial practices and procedures, and more.

Infrastructure relates to all of these, not just as separate ministries and operations, but in terms of how all these entities work together. For example, how they communicate and receive funding, how they train members to serve (to make it happen) and assimilate new people, and how they plan and execute their vision.

Infrastructure basically consists of two things: systems and people. Simply put, the *systems* are how things get done and the *people* are who gets them done. For instance, there is a system for how to check a child in and out of children's ministry, and there are people who make that system work, who care for the children and minister to them.

To the point, a church that has only built an infrastructure to facilitate an attendance of a thousand people can never grow to fifteen hundred people unless they first grow their infrastructure. They may touch fifteen hundred people on a special day—Easter, Christmas, the opening of a new worship center—but over time they will reduce to the level of their one-thousand-capacity infrastructure.

People talk about the new building bulge where they spike in attendance when they open a new worship center, but then they slowly migrate back to a point just over their previous average. The problem is, they built the new building for growth but did not build the infrastructure necessary to maintain it.

It's like a restaurant that fails to plan for a customer surge or a rush. There are plenty of open tables, but not enough hostesses, not enough food servers in the front room, not enough cooks in the back to accommodate that number of customers. And the systems break down due to the frantic nature of it all. Service is slow, the food is cold, and an otherwise wonderful experience is ruined for lack of infrastructure. The owners are thrilled at the crowd size and easily write off the mishaps as a few glitches, but they don't understand why customer retention is so low. The same is true of churches.

To prepare for and assimilate growth, a church should build its infrastructure for where they project (within reason) to be in their next stage of growth. If a church of 1,000 hopes to increase to 1,250, they need to build the infrastructure *now,* while they're at 1,000, to accommodate 1,250 people. To take the church to the next level, you must build the infrastructure as though you are already there, *before* you get there. It is clear, then, that growing a church and maintaining that growth is dependent on the constant growth of the church's infrastructure.

Of infrastructure's two aspects—systems and people—building the system side is so much easier than building the people side. While most people recoil at the thought of taking a few days and poring over policies, procedures, and processes, it can be done. Systems can be built almost overnight, but people are a slow build. It simply takes time to build people. Especially in a growing church, it always seems we are short on leaders. A well-structured, simple, but effective leadership-development pipeline is the key to continued growth.

A WELL-BUILT LEADERSHIP-
DEVELOPMENT PIPELINE

The pipeline is *not* called a leadership-development pipeline.

Before we get into the actual characteristics of a well-built leadership-development pipeline, we need to know up front that the pipeline should never be called the leadership-development pipeline. (You're thinking, *The whole book builds up to a discussion of the leadership-development pipeline, and the first thing you do is change its name. That's crazy!*) There are numerous reasons not to label it as such. We do not call our pipeline a leadership-development pipeline; we call it our *growth track*. Why didn't I simply start there? I wanted to establish that we're talking about developing leaders and avoid any confusion by differentiating from the other growth tracks in use in the body of Christ. Many churches use the term *growth track* to describe a variety of things. For some, it's a pathway, an introduction to the steps required for a believer to continually mature. I've actually seen a card that outlines one church's understanding of how key disciplines will lead believers down a path of growth. For others, the growth track is a series of classes that serves as an orientation for new members. Others use a growth track as a tool for connecting people to the local church. The list of variations on the use of the term *growth track* is almost endless. You can use whatever name you want for your pipeline, just don't call it a leadership-development pipeline.

You could call yours a leadership-development pipeline, but it wouldn't be the best decision you've ever made. First, no one wants to be in a pipeline. It sounds cold and impersonal. It sounds like you are mining for natural resources or processing business contacts. Second, most people do not see themselves as leaders and will deselect themselves from the process. To them, a leader is someone else, a person with a title, the person up front. People with that mind-set, which is the majority of people, will assume you are aiming for a subset of people that doesn't include them. But everyone wants to grow, which is why we call our leadership-development pipeline a growth track.

People naturally point to themselves: *my* life, *my* family, *my* money, *my* kids, *my* job, and so forth. They're more than happy to join a series of small groups that helps them find success and growth in these areas. But real success and growth are found in a life of complete devotion to Jesus and in service to others, a life where people discover their calling and begin to function in it. It's all about others, not about self, not about me and mine. So when a person joins our growth track, we begin to help them turn away from themselves as they commit to finding fulfillment in life through serving others.

A leadership pipeline is crucial to the perpetuation of a local church's culture. For that reason, it must be carefully and intentionally built. As we established in chapter 3, words give expression to ideas, ideas frame language, and language defines culture. A well-built pipeline gives developing leaders a language to match the culture they have been absorbing from the church environment. When they begin to hear the reasoning behind the process (those aha! moments that drive the concepts home), a leader then becomes a culture carrier.

For the rest of this chapter, I am going to use the terms *growth track* and *leadership-development pipeline* interchangeably to describe the systematic development of leaders in the local church.

Accessible

Actually, *accessible* is too soft a word. Encountering your growth track should be unavoidable. In our context, every person who attends any of our weekend services knows what their next step is within three minutes of worship ending. And they will hear something about the growth track every time we gather. It's part of the welcome portion of our service. Once guests and newcomers are welcomed (we do not embarrass guests by asking them to identify themselves), we explain that our goal is to help them grow, to become the people God intended them to be. We further explain that to help facilitate that growth, we have created a series of small groups we call the growth track. After a short summary of each step, we share a number of ways they can enter the growth track. (Our growth track small groups are called FirstStep, NextStep, and LeaderStep. Each will be described in terms of purpose and content later in this chapter.) Please note I said a "number of ways." Your growth track should be overwhelmingly accessible—unavoidable—and there should be multiple ways to connect with it.

I think people should hear about your growth track in each service. You can make it part of the initial public greeting, like we do. Personally, I like that idea because it establishes its value. What you say first and often (in our case every weekend) conveys your priority. Obviously, you *don't* have to talk about your growth track first thing out of the gate each week; you can vary when you communicate to attenders: during announcements, in the bulletin (if you use one), through video, testimonies, stories. Just make sure your growth track gets some platform exposure each week.

Whenever a sermon intersects with growth track content, seize that moment and mention it. You may interject something like, "You may remember this is a key point in our growth track" or "That's why we made this crucial concept a part of our growth track" or "You can see why it was so important we include this in our growth track" or "If you want more on this point, let me refer you to our growth track." Referencing the growth track in messages is another way to establish its priority. Sermon mentions always outweigh announcements in pushing something forward.

It doesn't do any good to tell people about the growth track if you don't also tell them how they can connect to it. We tell people each time we mention it that more information on and how to connect to a growth track small group are available on our website, on the Manna Church app, and at our growth track kiosk in the lobby of all of our sites. A site host may say something like, "Take out your smartphone, download the Manna app right now, click on 'Get Connected,' and join a growth track small group right now."

Perhaps our most effective method of connecting people to the growth track has nothing to do with a public announcement (although we would never consider not giving the growth track pulpit time). Our most effective method is shoulder tapping. Since the growth track is a series of small groups, many of our ministry lanes (worship, parking teams, coffee shop, outreach, greeters, and so forth) conduct growth track groups for the people on their SERVE teams. And if you think about it, that's a genius idea! What better way to ensure the lane you lead is constantly developing new leaders than developing them yourself?

For example, the leader of the 11:00 a.m. parking lot team at the Cliffdale site might run a LeaderStep small group for team members to prepare them to SERVE at the next level. The cool thing about this is that no one on our lead team suggested that lane leaders do this. Some lane leaders came up with this idea on their own. (That's another indication that a leadership-development culture exists and is empowering leadership development to happen on its own.)

Simple

When I was in Bible college, my pastor, Jerry Daley, said something that stuck with me: "Anyone can make simple things complicated; the real genius is in making complicated things simple." I never forgot that. If people have a hard time understanding what the growth track is, it will never develop the traction required to make it part of a local church's rhythm, part of the woodwork itself. It will always be viewed as an add on, something extra.

Our church is a small-group church, so it makes sense that the delivery system should be a series of small groups. Literally, everything in our church is a small group. The 9:30 a.m. greeting team at the Executive Place site is a small group. The elders are a small group. Find a delivery system that is already part of how your church operates. For example, if your meeting night is Wednesday night, and that's when the youth, college, and worship teams meet, as well as elders and deacons, you might consider absorbing your growth track into your midweek rhythm. Think about how people in your church already do things and insert your growth track right there.

Years ago I heard about a university that, tired of paving sidewalks only to have students destroy the grass by taking shortcuts across the lawns, decided to delay pouring sidewalks until the students established the walking patterns. Then they paved the sidewalks where the kids were already walking. Put your growth track on your church's sidewalks (metaphorically speaking).

Simple relates to what you do, but simple also relates to what you say. What you call your growth track is very important, as is the nomenclature you use to describe it. As I already mentioned, call your leadership-development pipeline what you will, just make sure it fits the culture of your church. (As we stated in chapter 3, every church has a culture.) Since building people *is* the job, calling our pipeline the growth track fits very nicely into our philosophical bent. You might decide on something like "Life at Grace" (meaning Grace Presbyterian Church) or "Growing in Faith" (at Faith Baptist) or "Connections" (at Connect Church—the small groups could be called Connect with God, Connect with One Another, Connect with Mission). You get the idea.

We talk a lot about taking your next step in our church. It's part of our leadership-development ideology. A leader is a person who is becoming who God called him or her to be. Becoming implies process, a series of steps. They are discovering their calling and beginning to walk into it. There is movement in our walk with God. He is taking us someplace, individually and collectively. We might say, "Your next step is always outside your comfort zone." Or "Your next step is often in the direction of something you fear or that intimidates you." Or "God is interested in your direction, not perfection, so just take one step toward Him." Therefore, we embraced the step motif in naming our growth track small groups. This keeps things simple, and our people already have an idea that their walk with God will require them to continually take a step. In using this terminology, we are putting these small groups on the sidewalk.

Make the on-ramp into your pipeline simple—pulpit exposure, website, app, shoulder tapping—but also make certain that your nomenclature is simple to grasp.

Culture-Creating Mechanism

Your pipeline, your growth track, is not only the result of a leadership-development culture, it is a *culture-creating mechanism*. A well-built growth track contains all of the key cultural elements of a local church, and its content is replete with culture-producing language. The growth track is where everyone gets on the same page, where everyone develops the same vocabulary, where everyone finds their place or at least their next step, where everyone is infused with the vision, where everyone discovers why we do what we do the way we do it, where everyone learns our values and understands why we only do the things that promote those values and why we don't do other things (many of which are good things) that run counter to those values.

Everyone who has visited a hospital knows what an IV

tube (intravenous tube) is. This needle-and-tubing apparatus is a delivery system for medication and nutrients to enter directly into the blood stream. A well-built leadership-development pipeline is like an IV, depositing your culture directly into the blood stream of your local church. Do not be tempted to build the content around the pastor's latest preaching emphasis or in reaction to what other churches are doing around the country. And do not make it a theology class (technically your church's culture is part of its ecclesiology). Carefully, prayerfully, build the content to further develop leaders, all the while imparting to them your culture so the leaders you develop become culture carriers themselves. When this routinely happens, your church has shifted into all-by-itself leadership-development status.

More than a Class

Leadership development is so much more than knowledge acquisition. It's life change, and life change happens in relationship with other people. (That's another reason we chose the small-group environment as the setting for our growth track.) Sure, knowledge—information—is part of that, but *only* part of that. Knowledge that is stored cognitively is great in an argument; you've got something to say. But God desires that truth work its way out into our lives.

In John 8:32, Jesus said, "Then you will know the truth, and the truth will set you free." Truth and knowing the truth were intended to change us, to shape our lives. In his prayer of repentance after his sin with Bathsheba, David lamented, "You delight in truth in the inward being" (Ps. 51:6 ESV). I see David admitting that the truth of God's Word had been in his head, but it had not shaped his heart—his "inward being." I read David's prayer to mean that David was saying one of the lessons he learned through this debacle was to apply truth: live it, follow it, obey it, and not just know it propositionally.

The longest distance in the planet, metaphorically speaking, is the eighteen inches between the head and the heart. Truth becomes ours when it makes that long trek from revelation to reality, from the head to the heart, and that happens best in the context of relationship. A young man may have read the greatest books on marriage, but putting all the insight to work after the wedding day is a different story. Knowing it is easy, but living it is another matter. It takes being married for that young man to figure out that he doesn't know what he knows!

Your pipeline must teach the truth, but it must do so in an environment that enhances relationships.

Group Setting

I have read extensively over the years on discipleship, and almost all of these authors stress the one-on-one aspects of discipleship. The idea is the disciple maker works with one individual of the same sex in a formal or semiformal context, often with some type of curriculum, with the goal of helping that individual live more closely the tenets of Scripture in whatever field they are studying: marriage, prayer, finances, Bible study, and so forth. I think that is awesome and biblical. And I would most definitely call that discipleship.

But Jesus was the best disciple maker in history, and He mentored His followers in a small group. I think that is because the interactions, questions, and struggles of one in the group affected the others in the group and gave Jesus opportunities to speak to them according to the need of the moment. I see the arguments as to who was greatest and questions as to why they couldn't cast out a demon, for example, as setups for teaching aimed at the heart. In Matthew 5–7, Jesus literally sat His disciples down and taught them the character of the kingdom and then spent three years working it into their lives.

My point here is not to make a definitive statement as to *the* biblical method of discipleship. I simply want to make a case for the idea that life change happens best in the context of community.

A well-built pipeline equips people to know and enables them to be known by others. It is about information, but not just about information. It's also about connection. At their best, mentoring and discipleship are messy, so your pipeline needs to be built in a way to facilitate relationships. You don't have to use a small-group setting, but you should structure the gatherings in a way that promotes connection. It could be argued that the people in the group have plenty of life-application opportunities in the regular interactions with others outside the group. I won't argue that. But there is another reason why group interaction is important.

Later, when I give a snapshot of how our growth track is structured, you'll see that the growth track is a wonderful opportunity for the people leading it to help guide group members into ministries and other groups where they might discover their next step. The group, the way it is set up, also gives the leaders an idea of each participant's probable character strengths and weaknesses. Maybe this one is gregarious but immature. This person is deep, mature, and ready to lead tomorrow. This other person has great insights but talks too much. This couple has severe marriage issues and would benefit from a small-group cycle or two in a marriage small group. These are great people, each one with a calling from God, each one in a different place in their journey. The personal insights gained by the leaders of the growth-track group will help them better SERVE the group's members.

There is one more important reason to build a community context into your pipeline. A pipeline built this way, where the leaders come to truly know those in the group, creates a shoulder-tapping dreamland! As people graduate from FirstStep, NextStep, and LeaderStep, SERVE team leaders and lane leaders are free to communicate with the leaders of the growth-track group about which individuals or couples might fit into their ministry lane. SERVE team leaders and lane leaders are able to attend the final gathering of the group and shoulder tap the potential leaders based on their interaction with the group's leaders. Potential leaders can be guided into the next step that is best for them. You can see how this personal interaction and hands-on care is preferable to the cold call of a mass appeal for volunteers.

Trains in Both Attitudes and Action

By attitudes I mean philosophy, as in your philosophy of ministry—or to be theological, your ecclesiology. Again, this does not mean teaching them your statement of faith. While that is good, one of the purposes of the pipeline is to help people see church the way you see church.

Are you an attractional church, built on a come-and-see premise? (That's the style of church where the weekend experience is designed to wow guests, mostly unchurched people, to come back, to the end that they eventually become Christ followers. The mission is in the building.) Are you a missional church built on a go-and-do premise? (That's the style of church where the weekend service is designed to equip people to impact the world and win people to Christ in the world around them. The mission begins just outside the church door.) Are you both? Are you an evangelical, Bible-teaching church? (By that I mean, the style of church whose focus is primarily as a teaching center, equipping people to know and therefore live the truth.) Are you a charismatic or Pentecostal church? (That's the style of church whose passion is to help people experience the reality of God.)

There are too many styles of church and combinations of styles to fully enumerate here, and that's not my purpose in writing. My point is, the growth track should help people own your church's values and love the why behind how you do church, provided that the culture created by those values is life-giving.

The pipeline should be designed to help them love how you see church (attitudes) but also love how you do church (actions). This is the place to teach the why of church and train them in the how of church. In other words, "This is *why* we do what we do, and this is the *way* we do what we do." You'll see both reflected in the content of our growth track later in this chapter. Bottom line, for a church to grow and stay healthy, there must be a high degree of consistency: things done a certain way every time and over time. This organizational discipline is a key to success.

It's easy to see how this can be accomplished in a business environment. Everyone is paid and is at your disposal during work hours. You can train them as much and as often as you want, and you can incentivize compliance through perks, bonuses, promotions, and raises.

How does one create organizational discipline in a voluntary association like the church? Build the growth track to equip people to see church like you see church and to do church the way you do church.

Creates Movement

A well-built pipeline moves people from one level to another, layering insight and application as they go. Again, that's why we use a series of steps in our format; it gives a connotation of movement and growth. And while the use of that nomenclature is not necessary in your context, the ideas behind it are important. Movement implies a direction. Layers and levels indicate that things are built on top of other things. Growth is almost always sequential—twenty pounds to twenty-five pounds, twenty-four inches to thirty inches—even if, at times, it is in reverse—two thousand members to fifteen hundred members.

When we tell people we want to help them grow, we are implying that we will help them move from where they are now to where they need to be for the next leg of their journey with God. No one wants to stay where they are. Almost everyone hopes for a better day. That's why they make New Year's resolutions, pack out gyms, initiate diets, and come back to church at the beginning of each year. An offer to people that leans in the direction of "We can't do the work for you, but we can equip you with the tools you need to move forward" is an attractive offer.

So build your pipeline with sequence in mind—this

builds upon that. Make sure that each stage is in some way connected to the last stage and builds toward the next stage. Each stage should introduce new ideas and prepare people for increasing levels of service. Avoid the temptation to make your growth track one long, continuous course. We have found that people like to start and stop and then start again. So while each stage should build toward another, it's a good idea to separate them into distinct segments or stages. This allows people to accomplish something—to win—and move forward. It leaves them with a positive attitude about themselves and the process. People are more likely to jump back in after a break if they feel good about their growth-track experience to date. The failure rate with one long course is simply too high.

Another great reason to build the stages sequentially but separately is the fact that people can complete a segment faster than they can grow, faster than they can assimilate and live the insight they have gained. I'll flesh this out as I describe how our growth track operates.

HOW WE OPERATE OUR GROWTH TRACK

The Format

For us, each growth-track small-group gathering is one hour long, divided roughly in half—thirty minutes for teaching and thirty minutes for interaction and discussion. As I mentioned earlier, this allows growth track leaders to get to know the participants so they can more accurately direct them toward the next step upon completion of the small group. In addition, it allows leaders to observe the participants and evaluate their interaction with others in order to evaluate a person's readiness for ministry. Each participant is given a booklet to enable them to follow along and take notes.

Groups begin with a greeting and move directly into the content after each person has signed in. What follows is a discussion and Q&A on the covered material. If some participants miss a session, they can make it up at a later date.

Empowering Others and Quality Control

We shoulder tap and train mature believers, people who are gifted to teach and who live the values and culture of our church to SERVE as growth-track small-group leaders. Potential leaders are apprenticed by growth-track small-group leaders, and they serve alongside active leaders as they teach, lead, and facilitate a group.

Each teaching segment is accompanied by a video. Small-group leaders watch the video and take notes to make sure they are as close to the video content as possible. If they are not comfortable that they can convey the teaching at a level that does justice to the content, they have the option of showing the video.

Sending leaders back to the video allows for quality control even after many generations of leaders passing the baton to others.

The Steps

Presently, our growth track consists of three steps, and while each step is unique, all three steps include our three values. We use triangles as part of our language to convey that our church is built around three big ideas derived from the Great Commandment and the Great Commission: love God, love one another, and love the world. These values find their practical outworking in the local church in that we only do three things:

- Inspiring worship services
- Life-giving small groups
- World-changing outreach

And we *only* do those *three* things!

Manna Church is a multisite church, and each site is free to offer the steps as often as they like and in whatever context works best—between services, during the evening, at the building, or in homes.

A person who completes FirstStep can take a short break or go directly into NextStep as he or she sees fit. Depending on the spiritual maturity of an individual, he or she may skip FirstStep and go directly into NextStep, since FirstStep is designed primarily for new believers. A person, however, must complete NextStep before going into LeaderStep.

1. FirstStep is a four-week small group designed for new believers or people who need a new foundation. By that we mean, many believers were never taught and therefore never grew proficient in the basics of the faith. (See appendix 1.)

2. NextStep is a four-week small group designed to get people on the same page. This is where we explain our vision and help people find their part in it. Week 4 is designed to allow for extended discussion as this is an ideal time for SERVE team leaders and lane leaders to visit the group to shoulder tap potential new team members. (See appendix 2.)

3. LeaderStep is an eight-week small group designed to enable people to understand and catch our culture (attitude) and learn core ministry skills. We introduce them to our definition of a leader, our twelve operational principles (culture statements), how to mentor others, the 360 mentoring model, and how to lead a small group. (See appendix 3.)

All this can sound and seem a little overwhelming. I have one more piece of advice to pass on—easily the most important in the book—that will set your mind at ease. Do not put this book down without reading the conclusion.

CONCLUSION

(DON'T PUT THIS BOOK DOWN WITHOUT READING THIS SIMPLE PIECE OF ADVICE!)

We have been working at building a leadership-development culture for more than thirty years, and our pipeline is simply the outgrowth of that pursuit. Had I read this book thirty years ago, I would have been thrilled and terrified at the same time. Where do you start? I have had the opportunity to talk to many leaders in different countries over the years, and I have often been asked, "If a pastor wanted to build a leadership-development culture and eventually build a pipeline to help facilitate that, where should he start?"

Here's my best advice. If I started over today, I would start where I started. In the introduction I talked about my little group. I would gather a little group and begin to pour my life into them weekly. Remember, slow is fast.

I wish I had this book back then! If I had, after I gathered my group, I would have my key leaders read this book and discuss with them where we are weak and where are we strong. I would work with them to distill our culture down to its core. I'd talk and pray over the question, are we happy with this culture? That's really important, because you already have a culture, and you have long been spreading it. So if you come to the conclusion that it needs to change, now is the time! Make sure that leadership development is deeply embedded in that culture, and create some language to facilitate that.

I would make sure we all agree on the proposition that building people *is* the job and secure from them a commitment to serve people to that end. I would slowly introduce the idea of shoulder tapping at leaders' gatherings and begin to shoulder tap as well so I could get really good at it.

I would meet with my hand-selected group every week, make notes about what I would like to see built into these people, imagine them as they one day will be, and reverse engineer the pipeline. I would resist the temptation to put it in its final form, give myself some leeway to experiment, and see what works.

So my advice is for you to pour your life into your little group. Use the tools you've found here, and before long, I'll be reading your book.

ACKNOWLEDGMENTS

Thank you, Jim Laffoon and Jerry Daley, for believing in a long-haired kid in an Alice Cooper T-shirt with a calling to full-time ministry.

Thank you, Manna Church, for letting a skinny twenty-six-year-old pastor learn as I led. Your patience with me and your commitment to advance the kingdom of God have inspired me. These thirty-plus years have been an exciting journey. I'm glad God called us on this road together.

Thank you, Christopher, Jonathan, Joseph, Lauren, Margaret, Stephen, Annie, and Samuel for being the captive audience to my "mad" (not angry) ramblings about life and success. You were my first and most important leadership development pipeline. You have been the delight of my life.

Thank you to my best friend and wife, Laura. I was smitten with you when I first laid eyes on you, and I have remained smitten these forty-plus years. You believed in me every step of the way. You make me better. (And you're a very handy editor!)

APPENDIX 1

FIRSTSTEP

WEEK 1: MY NEW LIFE

Welcome to FirstStep! (Overview)

This four-week small group is offered every month on Sundays at convenient times. FirstStep is the first of three small groups that together constitute Manna's growth track. The other two steps are:

- NEXTSTEP. You'll discover how Manna "does church," why we exist, what we are passionate about, where we are going, and how you can be part of this adventure. NextStep is also a four-week small group offered every month on Sundays at convenient times.
- LEADERSTEP. This small group will help you be more fully equipped to bring kingdom leadership and influence to your family, to your workplace, to your community, and

at Manna Church. This eight-week small group is offered on Sundays at convenient times. Please note that completion of NextStep and Manna's membership application process are prerequisites for participation in LeaderStep.

You are probably in FirstStep for one of three reasons: (1) you are new to the faith, (2) you are finding your way back to God, or (3) you simply want to strengthen your basic foundations in your relationship with God.

Whatever your reason, it's great that you are a part of this small group. We will be focusing on foundations—those fundamental principles that form the bedrock on which we are to build and sustain our spiritual lives for our entire lives.

Our goal for the next four weeks is to discover what a balanced, integrated, and healthy life of a disciple of Jesus looks like, specifically within the context of Manna Church.

MANNA'S "TRIANGLE"

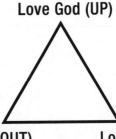

Love God (UP)

Love the World (OUT)   Love Each Other (IN)

FIRSTSTEP

Three Values, Six Applications, Nine Healthy Habits

THREE VALUES

Love God (Luke 10:27) **Week 2**
Love Each Other (Luke 10:27) **Week 3**
Love the World (Matt. 28:19–20) **Week 4**

SIX APPLICATIONS OF THE THREE VALUES

Love God: Inspiring Worship Experiences **Week 2**
1. Attend one
2. Serve at one

Love Each Other: Life-Giving Small Groups **Week 3**
1. Attend one
2. Lead one

Love the World: World-Changing Outreach **Week 4**
1. Bring others in
2. Go out

NINE HEALTHY HABITS

Love God: A Life of Devotion **Week 2**
1. Bible reading
2. Prayer
3. Worship (including tithing)

Love Each Other: It's All About Relationships **Week 3**
1. Fellowship
2. Accountability
3. Forgiveness

Love the World: Catching God's Heart for the Lost **Week 4**
1. Evangelism (witnessing: sharing your story)
2. Serving the needy
3. Generosity

The two people most responsible for your growth as a Christian are *Jesus* and *you!*

Now that we have outlined weeks two through four, let's spend the rest of week one thinking and talking about your story.

Your Story

- You have a story: who you *were*, who you *are*, who you are *becoming*.

> As for you, you were dead in your transgressions and sins, in which you used to live when you followed the ways of this world. But now in Christ Jesus you who once were far away have been brought near by the blood of Christ. (Eph. 2:1–2, 13)

Therefore, if anyone is in Christ, he is a new creation. The old has passed away; behold, the new has come. (2 Cor. 5:17 ESV)

To him who loves us and has freed us from our sins by his blood, and has made us to be a kingdom and priests to serve his God and Father—to him be glory and power for ever and ever! Amen. (Rev. 1:5–6)

We are God's handiwork, created in Christ Jesus to do good works, which God prepared in advance for us to do. (Eph. 2:10)

You show that you are a letter from Christ delivered by us, written not with ink but with the Spirit of the living God, not on tablets of stone but on tablets of human hearts. (2 Cor. 3:3 ESV)

I press on to take hold of that for which Christ Jesus took hold of me. (Phil. 3:12)

- You are to *share* your story.
  - Share to grow

I pray that your partnership with us in the faith may be effective in deepening your understanding of every good thing we share for the sake of Christ. (Philem. 1:6, emphasis added)

- Share to win

And they have conquered him [the Enemy] by the blood of the Lamb and *by the word of their testimony*, for they loved not their lives even unto death. (Rev. 12:11 ESV, emphasis added)

- Share to bless

Praise be to the God and Father of our Lord Jesus Christ, the Father of compassion and the God of all comfort, who comforts us in all our troubles, so that we can comfort those in any trouble with the comfort we ourselves receive from God. (2 Cor. 1:3–4)

Going Deeper
- Consider taking the time to start writing down your answers to the "Questions to Consider."
- What were you like before you became a Christian?
- Under what circumstances did you come to receive Jesus Christ as Lord and Savior?
- What changes has God brought to your life as you have yielded to and followed Him?

- What passions, purposes, goals, and plans has God brought to your life?
- What is God currently doing in your life?
- What are your strategies for effectively communicating your story to your family, friends, and coworkers?
- Resources
  - https://billygraham.org/grow-your-faith/how-to -share-your-faith/tools
  - https://billygraham.org/story/sharing-your-faith-101

WEEK 2: A LIFE OF DEVOTION

We believe that as you incorporate Manna's three values, six applications, and nine healthy habits into your life, your life will be transformed. These are fundamentals on which we build throughout our lives.

Our overall goal in FirstStep is to discover what a balanced, integrated, and healthy life of a disciple of Jesus looks like, specifically within the context of Manna Church.

In this session, we will explore important aspects of living a life devoted to God.

Value #1—Love God

Love the Lord your God with all your heart and with all your soul and with all your strength and with all your mind. (Luke 10:27 esv)

APPLICATIONS

Inspiring Worship Experiences

- **ATTEND ONE:** I don't mean attend one occasionally. Find the site and service that fits you and attend as often as you possibly can. You want to be in service every week—inclement weather, tired, feeling good or bad. Our job is to bring people into the proximity of the presence of God. It is in the presence of God our lives change.
- **SERVE AT ONE:** VIP team, worship team, children's ministry, or production. The SERVE team is a big team that includes all the other teams.

HEALTHY HABITS

"We first make our habits, and then our
habits make us." (anonymous)

1. Bible Reading: Engaging God's Word

You cannot get where you want to go in life without this Book. Everything you need for life is found in this Book. You want your marriage to change? It's here. You want a nation to change? It's here. Economics, war, joy, childrearing. It's all in the Bible.

Heaven and earth will pass away, but my words will
never pass away. (Matt. 24:35)

Man shall not live on bread alone, but on every *word* that comes from the mouth of God. (Matt. 4:4, emphasis added)

All Scripture is *God*-breathed and is useful for teaching, rebuking, correcting and training in righteousness, so that the servant of God may be thoroughly equipped for every good work. (2 Tim. 3:16–17, emphasis added)

Your word is a lamp to my feet, and a light to my path. (Ps. 119:105 ESV, emphasis added)

Do not merely *listen* to the word, and so deceive yourselves. *Do* what it says. (James 1:22, emphasis added)

Helpful ways to develop a healthy habit of engaging God's Word:

- LEARN from the Bible (from teachers, preachers, discussion in small groups).
- LISTEN to the Bible (online, audio Bibles, Bible apps).
- READ the Bible on your own (personal devotions, reading plans).
- READ the Bible with others (small groups, with family).
- MEMORIZE verses from the Bible.
- MEDITATE on verses from the Bible.
- OBEY what is written in the Bible!

2. *Prayer: Communicating with God*

Very early in the morning, while it was still dark, *Jesus* got up, left the house and went off to a solitary place, where he prayed. (Mark 1:35, emphasis added)

Call to me and I will *answer* you and tell you great and unsearchable things you do not know. (Jer. 33:3, emphasis added)

My sheep listen to my voice; I know them, and they follow me. (John 10:27)

Do not be anxious about anything, but in everything by prayer and supplication with thanksgiving [*thank you* are the two greatest words of faith] let your *requests* be made known to God. (Phil. 4:6 ESV, emphasis added)

Pray then like this: Our *Father* in heaven, hallowed be your name. Your kingdom come, your will be done, on earth as it is in heaven. Give us this day our *daily* bread, and *forgive* us our debts, as we also have forgiven our debtors. And lead us not into temptation, but *deliver* us from evil. (Matt. 6:9–13 ESV, emphasis added)

When you pray . . .

P **Praise God**

R **Repent**

A **Ask**

Y **Yield** (Your will, not mine)

E **Expect** (Expect to hear from Him and for Him to move in your life.)

R **Respond** (When He does, when He prompts you, respond to Him. Do what He tells you.)

3. Worship: Enjoying God

> "Worship is our response, both personal
> and corporate, to God for who He is, and
> what He has done; expressed in and by the
> things we say and the way we live."
> —Louie Giglio

Let everything that has *breath* praise the LORD! (Ps. 150:6 ESV, emphasis added)

Delight yourself in the LORD, and he will give you the desires of your heart. (Ps. 37:4 ESV, emphasis added)

I appeal to you therefore, brothers, by the mercies of God, to present your bodies as a living *sacrifice*, holy and acceptable to God, which is your spiritual worship. (Rom. 12:1 ESV, emphasis added)

Will man rob God? Yet you are robbing me. But you say, "How have we robbed you?" In your *tithes* and contributions. (Mal. 3:8 ESV, emphasis added)

"Devotion' to Christ is where the
human heart is most satisfied."
—Michael Fletcher,
Manna Church LeaderStep, week 2

Crucial to our growing in the above disciplines is our relationship with the Holy Spirit! We are all called to "be filled with the Spirit" (Eph. 5:18). For believers this simply means we are to be continually and increasingly surrendered to and dependent on the person and ministries of the Holy Spirit.

But the Advocate, the Holy Spirit, whom the Father will send in my name, will teach you all things and will remind you of everything I have said to you. (John 14:26)

When he, the Spirit of truth, comes, he will guide you into all the truth. He will not speak on his own; he will speak only what he hears, and he will tell you what is yet to come. He will glorify me because it is from me that he will receive what he will make known to you. (John 16:13–14)

If you then, though you are evil, know how to give good gifts to your children, how much more will your Father in heaven give the Holy Spirit to those who ask him! (Luke 11:13)

For more on the Holy Spirit's ministries, see Ephesians 6:18; Romans 8:26; Acts 1:8; Acts 2:1–4, 38–39; Acts 4:31; Acts 8:14–17; Acts 19:1–7.

Going Deeper

- What obstacles do you see to your establishing and strengthening a strong foundation in personal Bible reading, prayer, and worship?
- What simple, practical steps will you take to overcoming those obstacles?

WEEK 3: IT'S ALL ABOUT RELATIONSHIPS

Our overall goal in FirstStep is to discover what a balanced, integrated, and healthy life of a disciple of Jesus looks like, specifically within the context of Manna Church. In the last session, we talked about Bible reading, prayer, and worship. In this session, we will explore important aspects of living a life in which we learn to genuinely love one another.

Value #2—Love Each Other

You shall love your neighbor as yourself. (Matt. 22:39 ESV)

By this all people will know that you are my disciples, if you have love for one another. (John 13:35 ESV)

This is a core value. It is a core value for us; it is to be a core value for all Christians.

APPLICATIONS

Life-Giving Small Groups

We believe small groups are the perfect environment to learn to live out the next three healthy habits.

- **ATTEND A SMALL GROUP:** There are hundreds of options online on the Manna Church website or the Manna Church app.
- **LEAD A SMALL GROUP:** Use what God has put in your life and lead one yourself. Attend and complete LeaderStep! (Note: completing NextStep and becoming a member of Manna Church are prerequisites for LeaderStep.)

HEALTHY HABITS

1. Fellowship: Quality Time with Other Christians

The Acts 2 Model: write that in the margin of your FirstStep notebook.

They devoted themselves to the apostles' teaching and to *fellowship*, to the breaking of bread and to prayer. Everyone was filled with awe at the many wonders and signs performed by the apostles. All the believers were *together* and had everything in common. They sold property and possessions to give to anyone who had need. Every day they continued to meet *together* in the temple courts. They broke bread in their homes and ate *together* with glad and sincere hearts, praising God and enjoying the favor of all the people. And the Lord added to their number daily those who were being saved. (Acts 2:42–47, emphasis added)

And let us consider how we may spur one another on toward love and good deeds, not giving up meeting together, as some are in the habit of doing, but *encouraging* one another—and all the more as you see the Day approaching. (Heb. 10:24–25, emphasis added)

Do not be deceived: "Bad *company* ruins good morals." (1 Cor. 15:33 ESV)

2. Accountability: Being Real with Other Christians
It takes fellowship to have accountability.

As iron *sharpens* iron, so one person sharpens another. (Prov. 27:17, emphasis added)

Friction—sometimes you are intentionally looking for that friction. I want to be sharpened. I want to be sharp in my moral life. I want to be sharpened in my devotional life. I want to be sharpened in my marriage—losing weight, tongue.

I am going to find someone to hold me accountable.

> Therefore, *confess* your sins to one another and pray for one another, that you may be healed. The prayer of a righteous person has great power as it is working. (James 5:16 ESV, emphasis added)

> Two are better than one, because they have a good reward for their toil. For if they fall, one will lift up his fellow. But woe to him who is *alone* when he falls and has not another to lift him up! Again, if two lie together, they keep warm, but how can one keep warm alone? And though a man might prevail against one who is alone, two will withstand him—a three-fold cord is not quickly broken. (Eccl. 4:9–12 ESV)

Someone once said. "You're as sick as your secrets!" You need some folks who love you and know your secrets.

Important questions:

- Who in my life can hold me accountable?
- In what areas of my life do I need accountability?

(If you really want to grow, you have to take some steps here.)

3. Forgiveness: Trusting God with Our Pain
"When we refuse to forgive someone, it's like drinking *poison* and expecting the other person to die."

Let all bitterness and wrath and anger and clamor and slander be put away from you, along with all malice. Be kind to one another, tenderhearted, forgiving one another, as God in Christ *forgave* you. (Eph. 4:31–32 ESV, emphasis added)

Do not judge, and you will not be judged. Do not *condemn*, and you will not be condemned. Forgive, and you will be forgiven. (Luke 6:37, emphasis added)

Then Peter came to Jesus and asked, "Lord, how many times shall I forgive my brother or sister who sins against me? Up to seven times?" Jesus answered, "I tell you, not seven times, but *seventy-seven* times." (Matt. 18:21–22, emphasis added)

Bless those who curse you, pray for those who mistreat you. (Luke 6:28, emphasis added)

"A refusal to forgive means God stands back and lets you cope with your problems in your own strength."
—R. T. Kendall, from *Total Forgiveness*

- Ask God, "Who do I need to forgive?"
- Ask God to give you strength to choose to forgive and release them.
- Then forgive and release them.
- Just do it!

Going Deeper

- Ask the Lord to show you who you need to forgive. Make a list of the people, what they did (or didn't do) that hurt or offended you, and how their behavior impacted you.
- Choose to forgive each person for what they did and how it impacted you.
- Ask God to forgive you for harboring unforgiveness toward that person.
- Ask God to bring strength, healing, and restoration to the areas in which you were hurt.

WEEK 4: CATCHING GOD'S HEART FOR THE LOST

Our overall goal in FirstStep is to discover what a balanced, integrated, and healthy life of a disciple of Jesus looks like, specifically within the context of Manna Church. In this session, we will discuss loving the world. We will explore important aspects of living a life that catches God's heart for the lost.

Value #3—Love the World

For God so loved the world that he gave his one and only Son, that whoever believes in him shall not perish but have eternal life. (John 3:16)

Therefore go and make disciples of all nations. (Matt. 28:19)

APPLICATIONS

World-Changing Outreach

- BRING OTHERS IN: invite people in
- GO OUT: be outward focused. Advance the kingdom wherever you go. Pray for and look for opportunities to tell your story. Be involved in outreaches.

HEALTHY HABITS

1. Evangelism: Being a Witness by Telling Others About Jesus

By being willing to tell your story there will be times when the Holy Spirit prompts you to tell others about Jesus, to share your story.

Go into all the world and *proclaim* the gospel to the whole creation. (Mark 16:15 ESV, emphasis added)

But in your hearts honor Christ the Lord as holy, always being prepared to make a defense to anyone who asks you for a reason for the hope that is in you; yet do it with gentleness and respect. (1 Peter 3:15 ESV, emphasis added)

Have a relationship with Jesus (value #1), and He jumps right to value #3 by being ready to answer why you do what you do (why you follow Jesus). Examples:

For "everyone who calls on the name of the Lord will be saved." How then will they call on him in whom they have not believed? And how are they to believe in him of whom they have never heard? And how are they to hear without *someone* preaching? And how are they to preach unless they are sent? (Rom. 10:13–15 ESV, emphasis added)

But you will receive power when the Holy Spirit has come upon you, and you will be my *witnesses* in Jerusalem and in all Judea and Samaria, and to the end of the earth. (Acts 1:8 ESV, emphasis added)

What is your story? Be prepared to share parts of your story. See week 1 of FirstStep.

2. Serving the needy: Be a Witness by Showing Others the Love of Jesus
Evangelism = telling
Serving = showing

Let your light shine before men in such a way that
they may see your *good works*, and glorify your Father
who is in heaven. (Matt. 5:16 NASB, emphasis added)

Sometimes people need to hear the message, sometimes
people need to see the message.

For I was hungry and you gave me something to eat,
I was thirsty and you gave me something to drink, I
was a stranger and you invited me in, I needed clothes
and you clothed me, I was sick and you looked after
me, I was in prison and you came to visit me. . . .
Truly I tell you, whatever you did for one of the least
of these brothers and sisters of mine, you did for *me*.
(Matt. 25:35–36, 40, emphasis added)

Learn to *do good*; seek justice, correct oppression;
bring justice to the fatherless, plead the widow's cause.
(Isa. 1:17 ESV, emphasis added)

The church should help the needy, but also, the church should
step into the gap in the places of social injustice. The church's voice
should be heard where people are oppressed, the world should see
our manpower in these places as we all stand together.

Religion that God our Father accepts as pure and
faultless is this: to look after orphans and widows in

their *distress* and to keep oneself from being polluted by the world. (James 1:27, emphasis added)

Ways to serve those in need at Manna:

- small groups
- dream center
- outreach initiatives

So we love reaching the lost and serving those in need. Naturally, when you think about loving the Word, those two come to mind. But if we want to accomplish any of that, it is going to take giving from our resources.

3. Generosity: The Way to Get Is to Give

Remember this: Whoever sows sparingly will also reap sparingly, and whoever sows generously will also reap generously. Each of you should give what you have decided in your heart to give, not reluctantly or under compulsion, for God loves a *cheerful* giver. And God is able to bless you abundantly, so that in all things at all times, having all that you need, you will abound in every good work. [As I give, God will give back, As I sow, I will reap: "Once I see that I have your heart, and you get in the flow of this and give your time, talent and treasure, I know I can trust you and give you more."] As it is written: "They have freely scattered their gifts to the poor; their righteousness endures forever." Now he who supplies seed to the sower and bread for food [seed for the sower something to give, bread for food, something to keep for you.] You shouldn't give all that you have; some is for you. I will also supply and increase your store of seed and will enlarge the harvest of your righteousness. You will be enriched in every way so that you can be generous on every occasion, and through us your generosity will result in thanksgiving to God. (2 Cor. 9:6–11, emphasis added)

Don't eat your seed. He gives seed to the sower, but notice the order: He supplies as you sow. Many wait for supply before they sow, but it doesn't work that way—you sow first.

For the *love of money* is a root of all kinds of evil. Some people, eager for money, have wandered from the faith and pierced themselves with many griefs. (1 Tim. 6:10, emphasis added)

Remember Manna's Triangle: love God, love the world, love each other. If I really love God, I need to do what He calls me to do. God so loved the world that He *gave*. I am going to tell others, serve the poor, and then I am going to fund this. Some say, "But I love my money too much." Go back to value #1: some of how we worship God is with our money. It's about the heart. We want to have the same heart as God's.

> Give, and it will be given to you. Good measure, pressed down, shaken together, running over, will be put into your lap. For with the *measure* you use it will be measured back to you. (Luke 6:38 ESV, emphasis added)

The tithe is *returning* to God what is already His.

Giving *offerings* displays our generosity, as well as our commitment to advancing God's kingdom.

Going Deeper

- Is your attitude more focused on giving or on getting?
- Do you have financial peace? Do you have a working budget? Are you in debt?
- What are your strategies and plans to develop financial stability in your life?
- What and where are you sowing?
- How is God leading you to become more generous?

NEXT STEPS

- Become a member of the Manna Church family
- Attend and participate in NextStep
- Get involved in Manna's SERVE team

APPENDIX 2

NEXTSTEP

WEEK 1: WHO ARE WE?

The overall goal of NextStep is to discover the answers to the following questions:

- Who are we?
- Why are we here?
- Where are we going?
- What is my part?

In this session, we will be discussing, who are we?

"Everybody is somebody, but nobody is everybody."

Not all churches are called to emphasize the same things or "do church" in the same way. Each church family has its own unique calling from God.

We are not called to do everything. We are to discover, walk out, and fulfill our unique callings, and we are to fulfill those callings with excellence.

So, who are we?

A Vision to Change the World

We believe our Manna Church mission is to glorify God by equipping His people to change their world and by planting churches with a world-changing vision.

We plan to accomplish this by doing the following:

- Helping God's people discover their individual gifts and callings, creating an environment where these may be developed, and deploying God's people into their world to be salt and light. Our small groups are designed to help accomplish this goal.
- Helping God's people build strong families and creating a community where individuals may find fulfillment and expression regardless of age or marital status.
- Planting churches with the same vision both domestically and abroad.

Manna's Main Emphases

THE GREAT COMMANDMENT

But when the Pharisees heard that he had silenced the Sadducees, they gathered together. And one of them, a lawyer, asked him a question to test him. "Teacher, which is the great commandment in the Law?" And he said to him, "You shall love the Lord your God with all your heart and with all your soul and with all your mind. This is the great and first commandment. And a second is like it: You shall love your neighbor as yourself. On these two commandments depend all the Law and the Prophets." (Matt. 22:34-40 ESV)

THE GREAT COMMISSION

And Jesus came and said to them, "All authority in heaven and on earth has been given to me. Go therefore and make disciples of all nations, baptizing them in the name of the Father and of the Son and of the Holy Spirit, teaching them to observe all that I have commanded you. And behold, I am with you always, to the end of the age." (Matt. 28:18-20 ESV)

OUR APPLICATIONS

We do three things!

LOVE GOD: Inspiring Worship Experiences
LOVE EACH OTHER: Life-Giving Small Groups
LOVE THE WORLD: World-Changing Outreach

ONE CHURCH IN MANY LOCATIONS

- Church is people, not a place, a function, or a method.
- Church is anywhere and everywhere people gather in His name.
- If you want to multiply people, multiply groups.

MANNA CHURCH HAS DEVELOPED A "MULTIPLY STRATEGY" FOR REACHING THE WORLD

- At the beginning of human history, God gave us a mission: go forth and multiply. (Gen. 1:26–28; 15:1–7; 17:1–8).
- Of the early believers we read over and over how God multiplied their numbers greatly (Acts 6:7, 9:31, 12:24).
- *Multiply* is the math of God and happens when our "adds add."
- With a multiply strategy we can reach people anywhere and everywhere they can and will gather.

OUR MULTIPLY STRATEGY IS COMPRISED OF CITY SITES, MULTI- AND MICRO-SITES

- CITY SITE: a Manna Church location with 100–1,999 people in attendance for weekend experience(s); may have micro- or multi-site extensions
- MULTI-SITE: an extension of a city site

- **MICRO-SITE:** a gathering of people who are committed to glorifying God by helping to equip people to change their world. It embraces our three values and keeps our name, logo, and growth track. (Those who start and lead micro-sites will have been trained through another step in our growth track—MultiStep.)

MANNA'S "MILITARY HIGHWAY" STRATEGY

We plan to plant a city site or a micro-site near every US military base in the world, starting first with army bases. We also plan to plant city sites and micro-sites wherever people go when they leave military service or when they leave Fayetteville.

PAUL USED THE TECHNOLOGY OF HIS DAY TO REACH PEOPLE—LETTERS

Manna will use the technology of our day—video and the Internet.

BENEFITS OF MANNA'S MULTIPLY STRATEGY

- Multiply = more
- More leaders being developed
- More maturity in those who serve and receive
- More opportunities for members and guests to connect with our church
- More people being reached for Christ

WEEK 2: WHY ARE WE HERE?

In this session we will discuss the foundational *why* for Manna's existence.

We believe the primary, overarching purpose of the church is to demonstrate and advance the kingdom of God. The kingdom of God was Jesus' primary message. We believe it should also be ours.

We Start with the Dominion Mandate (Two Key Words)

> Then God said, "Let Us make man in Our image, according to Our likeness; and let them rule over the fish of the sea and over the birds of the sky and over the cattle and over all the earth, and over every creeping thing that creeps on the earth." God created man in His own image, in the image of God He created him; male and female He created them. God blessed them; and God said to them, "Be fruitful and multiply, and fill the earth, and subdue it; and rule over the fish of the sea and over the birds of the sky and over every living thing that moves on the earth." (Gen. 1:26–28 NASB)

TWO KEY WORDS

- "rule over" = *radah*: take dominion, or exercise authority over, everything (that you can see) that willingly submits itself to you

- "subdue" = *kabash*: take dominion, or exercise authority over, by force if necessary, everything that does not willingly submit itself to you

THE GARDEN OF EDEN: SATAN'S PLAN AND THE FALL OF MAN

- Satan wanted to steal the authority God had given man.
- When man fell, two things were lost:
  - Mankind: man came under the authority and influence of Satan.
  - Planet Earth

Did Satan's plan work? In a sense, yes. But God already had a plan of His own!

And I will put enmity between you and the woman, and between your offspring and hers; he will crush your head, and you will strike his heel. (Gen. 3:15)

In the days of those kings the God of heaven will set up a kingdom which will never be destroyed, and that kingdom will not be left for another people; it will crush and put an end to all these kingdoms, but it will itself endure forever. (Dan. 2:44 NASB)

Big question in Satan's mind: How was God going to try to crush him and the kingdom of darkness?

JESUS: THE DIVINE REVOLUTIONARY!

- He came to destroy the works of the Enemy
- Defeated (crushed) Satan at the cross
- Provided a way of freedom and salvation for those held captive
- Planted and established the kingdom

His Primary Message: the Kingdom of God
From that time on Jesus began to preach, "Repent, for the kingdom of heaven has come near." (Matt. 4:17)

From the days of John the Baptist until now, the kingdom of heaven has been subjected to violence, and violent people have been raiding it. (Matt. 11:12)

First time He ever uses the word *church*: Jesus will build a church that *advances* against and overcomes the gates of Hades (kingdom of darkness).

And Jesus said to him, "Blessed are you, Simon Barjona, because flesh and blood did not reveal this to you, but My Father who is in heaven. I also say to you that you are Peter, and upon this rock I will build My church; and the gates of Hades will not overpower it. I will give you the keys of the kingdom of heaven; and whatever you bind on earth shall have been bound in heaven, and whatever you loose on earth shall have been loosed in heaven." (Matt. 16:17–19 NASB)

WE ARE THE PLAN!

The kingdom Jesus established is to be advanced *through the church*!

Fear not, little flock, for it is your Father's good pleasure to give you the kingdom. (Luke 12:32 ESV)

So that the manifold wisdom of God might now be made known through the church to the rulers and the authorities in the heavenly places. This was in accordance with the eternal purpose which He carried out in Christ Jesus our Lord. (Eph. 3:10–11 NASB)

The purpose of the church is to advance the kingdom of God on the earth!

WEEK 3: WHERE ARE WE GOING?

Review

Manna's Mission Statement: We believe our Manna Church mission is to glorify God by equipping His people to change their world and by planting churches with a world-changing vision.

We plan to accomplish this by . . .

- Helping God's people discover their individual gifts and callings, creating an environment where these may be developed, and deploying God's people into their world to be salt and light. Our small groups are designed to help accomplish this goal.
- Helping God's people build strong families and creating a community where individuals may find fulfillment and expression regardless of age or marital status.
- Planting churches with the same vision both domestically and abroad.

On the way we are going to do three things:

LOVE GOD: Inspiring Worship Experiences
LOVE EACH OTHER: Life-Giving Small Groups
LOVE THE WORLD: World-Changing Outreach

Question: Who is the "we"?

Foundational Scriptures for Manna Church

And He gave some as apostles, and some as prophets, and some as evangelists, and some as pastors and teachers, for the equipping of the saints for the work of service, to the building up of the body of Christ; until we all attain to the unity of the faith, and of the knowledge of the Son of God, to a mature man, to the measure of the stature which belongs to the fullness of Christ. As a result, we are no longer to be children, tossed here and there by waves and carried about by every wind of doctrine, by the trickery of men, by craftiness in deceitful scheming; but speaking the truth in love, we are to grow up in all aspects into Him who is the head, even Christ, from whom the whole body, being fitted and held together by what every joint supplies, according to the proper working of each individual part, causes the growth of the body for the building up of itself in love. (Eph. 4:11–16 NASB)

And Jesus said to him, "Blessed are you, Simon Barjona, because flesh and blood did not reveal this to you, but My Father who is in heaven. I also say to you that you are Peter, and upon this rock I will build My church; and the gates of Hades will not overpower it. I will give you the keys of the kingdom of heaven; and whatever you bind on earth shall have been bound in heaven, and whatever you loose on earth shall have been loosed in heaven." (Matt. 16:17–19 NASB)

If my people, who are called by my name, will humble themselves and pray and seek my face and turn from their wicked ways, then will I hear from heaven, and I will forgive their sin and will heal their land. (2 Chron. 7:14)

The LORD will be awesome [terrifying to them] against them; for he will famish [starve] all the gods of the earth, and to him shall bow down, each in its place, all the lands of the nations. (Zeph. 2:11 ESV)

With my great power and outstretched arm, I made the earth and its people and the animals that are on it, and I give it to anyone I please. (Jer. 27:5)

So, given who we are, why we are, and where we are going, what's *your* next step?

WEEK 4: WHAT IS MY PART?

If the Bible is a sentence, and Jesus is the subject, what is the verb?

For God so loved the world that he gave his one and only Son, that whoever believes in him shall not perish but have eternal life. (John 3:16)

Perhaps *love* is the verb of the Bible?

- Essence of love = give without condition
- Counterfeit of love = lust, get, take
- Essence of love = give
- "For God so loved the world that He—" (what action?) *Gave!*

Give cuts across the root of our sin problem, which is self. When we give, we crucify self, act as God would, and set ourselves up to be blessed by Him in powerful and unexpected ways.

So if there is any encouragement in Christ, any comfort from love, any participation in the Spirit, any affection and sympathy, complete my joy by being of the same mind, having the same love, being in full accord and of one mind. Do nothing from selfish ambition or conceit [self], but in humility [give] count others more significant than yourselves [give]. Let each of you look not only to his own interests [self], but also to the interests of others [give]. Have this mind among yourselves, which is yours in Christ Jesus, who, though he was in the form of God, did not count equality with God a thing to be grasped [self], but emptied himself [give], by taking the form

of a servant [give], being born in the likeness of men
[give]. And being found in human form, he humbled
himself [give] by becoming obedient to the point of
death, even death on a cross [give]. Therefore God
has highly exalted him [result] and bestowed on him
the name that is above every name [result], so that at
the name of Jesus every knee should bow, in heaven
and on earth and under the earth, and every tongue
confess that Jesus Christ is Lord, to the glory of God
the Father [result]. (Phil. 2:1–11 ESV)

What happens when we "give"?

- Love
- Invest
- Store up treasure
  Do not lay up for yourselves treasure on earth,
  where moth and rust destroy and where thieves
  break in and steal, but lay up for yourselves treasures
  in heaven, where neither moth nor rust destroys
  and where thieves do not break in and steal. For
  where your treasure is, there your heart will be also.
  (Matt. 6:19–21 ESV)
- Empower
  But he, desiring to justify himself [self], said to
  Jesus, "And who is my neighbor?" Jesus replied, "A

man was going down from Jerusalem to Jericho, and he fell among robbers, who stripped him and beat him and departed, leaving him half dead. Now by chance a priest was going down that road, and when he saw him he passed by on the other side [self]. So likewise a Levite, when he came to the place and saw him, passed by on the other side [self]. But a Samaritan, as he journeyed, came to where he was, and when he saw him, he had compassion [love]. He went to him and bound up his wounds [give], pouring on oil and wine [give]. Then he set him on his own animal [give] and brought him to an inn and took care of him. And the next day he took out two denarii and gave them to the innkeeper, saying, 'Take care of him, and whatever more you spend, I will repay you [give] when I come back.' Which of these three, do you think, proved to be a neighbor to the man who fell among the robbers?" He said, "The one who showed him mercy [gave]." And Jesus said to him, "You go, and do likewise." (Luke 10:29–37 ESV)

- Partnership
- As followers of Jesus, we can give in three ways:
    - Time = serve
    - Talent = leading or participating in small groups
    - Treasure = finances

- Tithe = first 10 percent of your increase
- Offerings = as God or your heart leads you (We have a special outreach offering every year called the Advance the Kingdom Offering.)
- Alms = in service of the poor

You are not your own, for you were bought with a price. So glorify God in your body. (1 Cor. 6:19b–20 ESV)

Action Steps

See your site's "Next Steps After NextStep" handout.

- Become a member of Manna Church (if you haven't done so already)!
- Take LeaderStep (must have completed Manna membership process and NextStep)
- We want you on our SERVE team! VIP and host teams, WorldChangers children's ministries, production ministries, worship team, outreach and missions, Manna student ministries

So, what's *your* next step?

APPENDIX 3

LEADERSTEP

LeaderStep will help you be more fully equipped to demonstrate kingdom leadership and influence in your family, in your workplace, in your community, and at Manna Church. This eight-week small group is offered at convenient times on Sunday.

WEEK 1: WELCOME TO LEADERSTEP, MANNA'S PHILOSOPHY OF LEADERSHIP DEVELOPMENT

Quick Review

A VISION TO CHANGE THE WORLD

We believe our Manna Church mission is to glorify God by equipping His people to change their world and by planting churches with a world-changing vision.

We Plan to Accomplish This By . . .

- Helping God's people discover their individual gifts and callings, creating an environment where these may be developed, and deploying God's people into their world to be salt and light. Our small groups are designed to help accomplish this goal.
- Helping God's people build strong families and creating a community where individuals may find fulfillment and expression, regardless of age or marital status.
- Planting churches with the same vision both domestically and abroad.

We do three things:

LOVE GOD: Inspiring Worship Experiences
LOVE EACH OTHER: Life-Giving Small Groups
LOVE THE WORLD: World-Changing Outreach

MANNA'S "TRIANGLE"

Love God (UP)

Love the World (OUT)   **Love Each Other (IN)**

Multiply Strategy: One Church in Many Locations

Our effectiveness in fulfilling our calling as a church family depends in large part on developing a *leadership culture,* which grows all kinds of leaders within a wide variety of spheres of influence.

Question: Are leaders born or made?
The right answer is both.

- You can develop your leadership; God is prompting you to do so.
- Remember: You *are* a leader!
- Your development is more about your capacities, your character, and your faith being stretched and expanded than it is about acquiring knowledge and skills (though, of course, the latter *are* important). LeaderStep lays a vital foundation for your development as a leader, especially within the context of Manna Church.

Five Ideas

1. Everyone has a calling. God determined it.

I therefore, a prisoner for the Lord, urge you to walk in a manner worthy of the calling to which you have been called, with all humility and gentleness, with patience, bearing with one another in love, eager to maintain the unity of the Spirit in the bond of peace. There is one body and one Spirit—just as you were called to the one hope that belongs to your call. (Eph. 4:1–4 ESV)

2. Everyone has a set of gifts. God downloaded them.

As each has received a gift, use it to serve one another, as good stewards of God's varied grace. (1 Peter 4:10 ESV)

- You don't *determine* your gifts. Your job is to *discover* and *deploy* them.

3. Everyone has a set of talents and abilities. God decided on those.

- For ideas 1–3, get moving: you can't steer a parked car.

4. Everyone has a certain character cap. God gives opportunities for you to change that.

People are hard to work for.
People are hard to work with.
People are hard to lead.
Hurt people hurt people.

5. But Jesus died for people; that makes people the most valuable thing on the planet.

- People can change if they come into contact with the God who made them. Someone must lead them there.
- Leading people is the most rewarding thing in the world because:
  - These people belong to God. He has a plan for each one of their lives.
  - He has a special reward for those who lead them on His behalf.

So I exhort the elders among you, as a fellow elder and a witness of the sufferings of Christ, as well as a partaker in the glory that is going to be revealed: shepherd the flock of God that is among you, exercising oversight, not under compulsion, but willingly, as God would have you; not for shameful gain, but eagerly; not domineering over those in your charge, but being examples to the flock. And when the chief Shepherd appears, you will receive the unfading crown of glory. (1 Peter 5:1–4 ESV)

Insights from these verses from 1 Peter 5:

- "among" = those people with whom you are presently associated (this is tough because they know you best)
- "shepherd" = not the boss but a caretaker. You are the shepherd of the people.
- "oversight" = servanthood. Servanthood makes you great!

- "willingly" = not for gain. We don't do to *get*. We do to *give*. Getting comes later in a variety of forms—promotion (greater responsibility) or reward (here or in heaven).

Leadership lessons and character development occur best in . . .

- Any leadership opportunity, not just your *ideal* one. (Struggle is good!)
- Places that are over your head. ("If you're ready, you're late.")
- Circumstances where there are potential conflicts.
- Situations where you are uncomfortable.
- Places where you face failure. (Failure is not fatal, so take some risks!)
- Situations where you feel a deep need for God. God *wants* you there.

Five Practices of a Manna Leader

See and Shape the Future.	Catch the Vision!
Engage and Develop Others.	Believe in Others!
Reinvent Continually.	Always Improve!
Value Relationships *and* Results.	People *and* Performance!
Embody the Values.	Walk Your Talk!

We want you on our SERVE team!

Going Deeper

- What do you believe are your God-given callings, gifts, talents, and abilities? In what contexts are you developing (or would like to develop) these callings, gifts, talents, and abilities?
- What difficult life situations helped develop you as a person and as a leader? How did you respond to those situations to take advantage of these opportunities for growth?

WEEK 2: MANNA'S OPERATIONAL PRINCIPLES—DECODING OUR DNA, PART 1

Every church has its own unique calling, culture, personality, philosophy of ministry, and way of "doing church." Each church has its own DNA.

- Manna's DNA is expressed by our Twelve Operational Principles.
- Our culture is developed by our understanding and ongoing application of these principles.

Manna Church's Twelve Operational Principles:

1. The Bible is the handbook for life.
2. Devotion to Christ is the place where the human heart is most satisfied.
3. The presence of God is a person.

4. Choose character over charisma and anointing.
5. The church *is* the point.
6. The church is people, not a building.
7. The church is a force.
8. The church is not just a teaching center; it's a training center.
9. The church was intended to be a church without walls.
10. We are not a church with small groups; we are a small-group church.
11. Outreach is the heartbeat of church.
12. Excellence is the standard.

1. The Bible Is the Handbook for Life

Heaven and earth will pass away, but my words will not pass away. (Luke 21:33 ESV)

Your word is a lamp to my feet and a light to my path. (Ps. 119:105 ESV)

- PERSONAL LIFE: marriage, child rearing, personal finance, sin, and forgiveness
- SOCIAL AND GOVERNMENT LIFE: justice, not the type of government but the role of civil authority
- CHURCH LIFE: what Jesus had in mind when He created the church.

Some people say, "Yes, we believe in the Bible, but when it comes to the issues of life—how to discipline our children, how to build our marriages, discussions on abortion or homosexuality, how to build the church—we need to use our own common sense in this modern context."

The Bible will be around long after our good ideas are gone. This doesn't mean we can't use our brains. This means we *begin* here with the Bible!

2. Devotion to Christ Is the Place Where the Human Heart Is Most Satisfied

THE FIRST COMMANDMENT COMES BEFORE THE GREAT COMMISSION

You shall love the LORD your God with all your heart and with all your soul and with all your might. (Deut. 6:5 ESV)

Love the Lord your God with all your heart and with all your soul and with all your mind and with all your strength. (Mark 12:30 ESV)

For His divine power has bestowed on us everything necessary for a dynamic spiritual life and godliness, through true and personal knowledge of

Him who called us by His own glory and excellence. (2 Peter 1:3 AMP)

3. The Presence of God Is a Person—He Is the Holy Spirit

Throughout all their journeys, whenever the cloud was taken up from over the tabernacle, the people of Israel would set out. But if the cloud was not taken up, then they did not set out till the day that it was taken up. For the cloud of the LORD was on the tabernacle by day, and fire was in it by night, in the sight of all the house of Israel throughout all their journeys. (Ex. 40:36–38 ESV)

Nevertheless, I tell you the truth: it is to your advantage that I go away, for if I do not go away, the Helper will not come to you. But if I go, I will send him to you. And when he comes, he will convict the world concerning sin and righteousness and judgment. (John 16:7–8 ESV)

When the Spirit of truth comes, he will guide you into all the truth, for he will not speak on his own authority, but whatever he hears he will speak, and he will declare to you the things that are to come. He will glorify me, for he will take what is mine and declare it to you. (John 16:13–14 ESV)

But you will receive power when the Holy Spirit comes on you; and you will be my witnesses in Jerusalem, and in all Judea and Samaria, and to the ends of the earth. (Acts 1:8)

Truly, truly, I say to you, whoever believes in me will also do the works that I do; and greater works than these will he do, because I am going to the Father. (John 14:12 ESV)

If you then, though you are evil, know how to give good gifts to your children, how much more will your Father in heaven give the Holy Spirit to those who ask him! (Luke 11:13)

For more on the Holy Spirit's ministries, see Ephesians 5:18, Romans 8:26, Acts 2:1–4, Acts 2:38–39, Acts 4:31, Acts 8:14–17, Acts 19:1–7, 1 Corinthians 12 and 14.

4. Choose Character over Anointing

Many people are enamored with and attracted to talent, gifts, and anointing; in some cases, beguiled by them. Without character, it will all fall apart. We are not against talent, anointing, and the like, but character trumps those.

Neither Manna nor Paul are against spiritual gifts. It is just that spiritual gifts don't make you spiritual; character does (one of the themes in 1 Corinthians).

- In 1 Timothy and Titus, Paul outlines qualifications for elders and deacons. Every point is about character. He says nothing on spiritual gifts, nothing on anointing, and only one thing on abilities—that you should be able to teach. (He doesn't even say you have to be good at it!)
- Anointing can be cooked in the microwave, but character only cooks in a Crock-Pot.
- Brokenness, humility, loyalty, faithfulness, integrity, standing by your word, generosity, kindness, sacrifice, perseverance, love—these are the things that make people spiritual.

Going Deeper

- What is your attitude toward the Bible? How have you grown in your appreciation of the authority of Scripture?
- In what practical ways are you cultivating your personal devotion to Jesus Christ?
- In what ways do you depend on the person and ministries of the Holy Spirit? How are you experiencing His ministry in and through your life?
- What circumstances has God brought you through that developed your character so that your gifts, talents, and abilities were more effective for the kingdom?

WEEK 3: MANNA'S OPERATIONAL PRINCIPLES—DECODING OUR DNA, PART 2

5. The Church Is the Point

- God always was and is about *people.*
- Mankind fell, and God provided salvation for them.
- Those He saved are called the church, whom He loves. "She will bear a son, and you shall call his name Jesus, for he will save his people from their sins." (Matt. 1:21 ESV)
- He rules the whole universe in relation to His people, the church. (The whole Old Testament is about His ruling over and dealing with the nations in relation to His people. The book of Revelation is about His ruling in relation to the church.)

And when he had taken the scroll, the four living creatures and the twenty-four elders fell down before the Lamb, each holding a harp, and golden bowls full of incense, which are the prayers of the saints. And they sang a new song, saying, "Worthy are you to take the scroll and to open its seals, for you were slain, and by your blood you ransomed people for God from every tribe and language and people and nation, and you have made them a kingdom and priests to our God, and they shall reign on the earth." (Rev. 5:8–10 ESV)

- Governments, corporations, and entertainers are not the point. They are part of the world, but the real point—the primary focus—of all that God is doing is the church, His people.

6. The Church Is People, Not a Building

Many churches think "church" is what happens when we meet or is synonymous with the place in which we meet. In this view everything about church centers on the building, and those who do ministry and who control ministry are the professional leaders. Volunteers are recruited to ministry, which means (is synonymous with) keeping the programs of the church running. The center of ministry is the church building.

- We believe the church is people, and ministry happens through you in the place where you live. The role of the *professional* clergy is to equip and coach the people. Our job is to create an environment where people may become who God has called them to become.

You yourselves like living stones are being built up as a spiritual house, to be a holy priesthood, to offer spiritual sacrifices acceptable to God through Jesus Christ. (1 Peter 2:5 ESV)

And he gave the apostles, the prophets, the evangelists, the shepherds and teachers, to equip the saints for the work of ministry, for building up the body of Christ. (Eph. 4:11–12 ESV)

- Traditional church = the people are in the stands, and the *professionals* play the game.
- Our view = the people are on the field, the professionals coach, and the "great cloud of witnesses" is in the stands.
- We believe in *people*. So we often have more faith for people than they have for themselves.

7. The Church Is a Force

- Inward churches see the church as a field—the focus of ministry, the place where ministry is done.
- Outward churches see the world as the field and the church (the people) as the force.
- Our mission statement does not use *minister* as the core action verb, but *equip*.
- Ministry is available here because people are equipped to do it.
- Small groups provide a perfect environment for people to discover, develop, and deploy their individual giftedness and callings.
- People are called to reach their world.
  - Bed = where you live, your spheres of influence

And He made from one man every nation of mankind to live on all the face of the earth, having determined their appointed times and the boundaries of their habitation. (Acts 17:26 NASB)

- Buck = your occupation—work, school
- Burden = your passions, causes

8. The Church Is Not Just a Teaching Center; It's a Training Center

- People grow best in a grace-filled environment, so create a place where failure is not fatal.
- We are a permission-granting, not a permission-withholding institution.
- Religious control is a form of wickedness. Leadership is given by God to equip and empower people to operate in their callings.

  And he gave the apostles, the prophets, the evangelists, the shepherds and teachers, to equip the saints for the work of ministry, for the building up the body of Christ. (Eph. 4:11–12 ESV)

- Generosity is our default. If you are going to err, always err on the side of generosity.
- Grace is more than just a gift and certainly more than a doctrine; it is a lifestyle.
  - *Grace* does not mean "soft on sin." Grace without justice is not grace. Love *and* truth must exist together for either to remain balanced.
- We believe in people.

WEEK 4: MANNA'S OPERATIONAL PRINCIPLES—DECODING OUR DNA, PART 3

9. *The Church Was Intended to Be a Church Without Walls*

- It should not have to be said that God is the Creator and His creation is beautiful. He created, and therefore loves, diversity.

- Division by race, socioeconomic status, fame, or intellect is unbiblical. God is no respecter of persons. We do not *accept* African-Americans, Hispanics, Asians, or Whites because they are Christian African Americans, Hispanics, Asians, and Whites. We don't *look past* their race, saying, "I don't even think of you as a white person/black/Latino." Just the opposite: "I do think of you as white/black/Latino because that is who you are, and I love you as you are."

For he himself is our peace, who has made us both one and has broken down in his flesh the dividing wall of hostility by abolishing the law of commandments expressed in ordinances, that he might create in himself one new man in place of the two, so making peace, and might reconcile us both to God in one body through the cross, thereby killing the hostility. (Eph. 2:14–16 ESV)

If anyone says, "I love God," and hates his brother, he is a liar; for he who does not love his brother whom he has seen cannot love God whom he has not seen. (1 John 4:20 ESV)

All this is from God, who through Christ reconciled us to himself and gave us the ministry of reconciliation; that is, in Christ God was reconciling the world to himself, not counting their trespasses against them, and entrusting to us the message of reconciliation. (2 Cor. 5:18–19 ESV)

- The church is a place of healing and reconciliation. Therefore, it is an institution that is without walls. Religion builds walls to keep "good" people in and "bad" people out. Christianity tears down walls and seeks to deliver the healing message of the gospel to all who need it.
- There is order and discipline in the church, but the doors of the church (people's hearts) are always open to others who are outside.

10. We Are Not a Church with Small Groups; We Are a Small-Group Church
- We see that the church in the New Testament includes both *celebration* and *cell*—in our context, Sunday morning and small groups.
- Acts 2 Model

They were continually devoting themselves to the apostles' teaching and to fellowship, to the breaking of bread and to prayer. Everyone kept feeling a sense of awe; and many wonders and signs were taking place through the apostles. And all those who had believed were together and had all things in common; and they began selling their property and possessions and were sharing them with all, as anyone might have need. Day by day continuing with one mind in the temple, and breaking bread from house to house, they were taking their meals together with gladness and sincerity of heart, praising God and having favor with all the people. And the Lord was adding to their number day by day those who were being saved. (Acts 2:42–47 NASB)

- They learned this from Jesus. This is how He operated in the Gospels and how He instructed His disciples to operate.
- *Oikos* = "household," your sphere of influence. Everyone has one. You are the light to them. You are their pastor.

The next day again John was standing with two of his disciples, and he looked at Jesus as he walked by and said, "Behold, the Lamb of God!" The two disciples heard him say this, and they followed

Jesus. Jesus turned and saw them following and said to them, "What are you seeking?" And they said to him, "Rabbi" (which means Teacher), "where are you staying?" He said to them, "Come and you will see." So they came and saw where he was staying, and they stayed with him that day, for it was about the tenth hour. One of the two who heard John speak and followed Jesus was Andrew, Simon Peter's brother. He first found his own brother Simon and said to him, "We have found the Messiah" (which means Christ). He brought him to Jesus. Jesus looked at him and said, "You are Simon the son of John. You shall be called Cephas" (which means Peter). The next day Jesus decided to go to Galilee. He found Philip and said to him, "Follow me." Now Philip was from Bethsaida, the city of Andrew and Peter. Philip found Nathanael and said to him, "We have found him of whom Moses in the Law and also the prophets wrote, Jesus of Nazareth, the son of Joseph." (John 1:35–45 ESV)

- All of life is about relationships. Our small groups should help facilitate relationships directly (friendship) or indirectly through teaching and mentoring (marriage, child-rearing).
- Everything in our church is a small group.

11. Outreach Is the Heartbeat of "Church"

- Outreach is not an option; it is a mandate. The Great Commandment ("love the Lord your God") is followed by the Great Commission.

And Jesus came and said to them, "All authority in heaven and on earth has been given to me. Go therefore and make disciples of all nations, baptizing them in the name of the Father and of the Son and of the Holy Spirit, teaching them to observe all that I have commanded you. And behold, I am with you always, to the end of the age." (Matt. 28:18–20 ESV)

But you will receive power when the Holy Spirit has come upon you, and you will be my witnesses in Jerusalem and in all Judea and Samaria, and to the end of the earth. (Acts 1:8 ESV)

And Saul approved of his execution. And there arose on that day a great persecution against the church in Jerusalem, and they were all scattered throughout the regions of Judea and Samaria, except the apostles. Devout men buried Stephen and made great lamentation over him. But Saul was ravaging the church, and entering house after house, he dragged off men and women and committed them to prison. Now those who were scattered went about preaching the Word. (Acts 8:1–4 ESV)

- Jesus died for real people and sent real people to reach them.
- Our best testimony is life well lived.
- People need to be equipped to understand their life messages, be comfortable sharing the gospel, and confident in the faith they are living.
- Outreach includes every part of the globe and every people group on the planet. We are especially drawn to the most difficult and dangerous people groups. Perhaps it is the redemptive call on the city of Fayetteville, but we say yes to the mission before considering financial cost or personal safety.
- The church is the vehicle to advance the kingdom of God on planet Earth.
- Growth and success are expected. At the same time, we fear neither risk nor failure. Our expectation is simply this: once we see the vision He reveals and set our hearts to work fearlessly toward that end, He will provide the results He intended for us to have.
- Stick to the vision and work the plan. We can't do everything, so let's do what we are called to do really well.

- Ultimately every church really has the same calling. We plan to do our part in the way that God has called us to do it. And every step of the way, that plan includes you!

12. Excellence Is Our Standard

Whatever you do, work at it with all your heart, as working for the Lord, not for human masters, since you know that you will receive an inheritance from the Lord as a reward. It is the Lord Christ you are serving. (Col. 3:23–24)

- Excellence = relentless improvement
- Manna's worship experiences are designed to honor God, engage people, and portray a spirit of excellence befitting the worship of our awesome God.
- That same spirit of excellence should extend to everything we do.
- Balance! We are not talking about perfection! Pay attention to the Law of Diminishing Returns, which says as you add elements, the overall quality can tend to decrease.

WEEK 5: OUR PHILOSOPHY OF SMALL GROUPS

Life change happens in the context of relationships.
Small groups are biblical.

Making disciples is our mandate, so we need a plan. Jesus modeled this for us by gathering twelve men around Him and teaching them in the context of everyday living. The early church expanded on this method.

All authority has been given to Me in heaven and on earth. Go therefore and make disciples of all nations, baptizing them in the name of the Father and the Son and the Holy Spirit, teaching them to observe all that I commanded you; and lo, I am with you always, even to the end of the age. (Matt. 28:18–20 NASB)

They devoted themselves to the apostles' teaching and to fellowship, to the breaking of bread and to prayer. Everyone was filled with awe at the many wonders and signs performed by the apostles. All the believers were together and had everything in common. They sold property and possessions to give to anyone who had need. Every day they continued to meet together in the temple courts. They broke bread in their homes and ate together with glad and sincere hearts, praising God and enjoying the favor of all the people. And the Lord added to their number daily those who were being saved. (Acts 2:42–47)

And He gave some as apostles, and some as prophets, and some as evangelists, and some as pastors and teachers, for the equipping of the saints for the work of service, to the building up of the body of Christ; until we all attain to the unity of the faith, and of the knowledge of the Son of God, to a mature man, to the measure of the stature which belongs to the fullness of Christ. As a result, we are no longer to be children, tossed here and there by waves and carried about by every wind of doctrine, by the trickery of men, by craftiness in deceitful scheming; but speaking the truth in love, we are to grow up in all aspects into Him who is the head, even Christ, from whom the whole body, being fitted and held together by what every joint supplies, according to the proper working of each individual part, causes the growth of the body for the building up of itself in love. (Eph. 4:11–16 NASB)

A Manna Church small group consists of three or more people who gather to build community, to grow and serve together. Manna small groups provide an environment in which people can (1) grow in their relationship with Jesus and (2) discover and develop their God-given passions, giftings, and talents. These groups can meet in homes, coffee shops, restaurants, church buildings, or other places.

People need people to grow into all God has for them.

APPENDIX 3

Why "Free Market" Small Groups?

- It capitalizes on who you are. it provides a culture that allows for freedom of expression, opportunity, and creativity.
  - Your interests, passions, and burdens
  - Your abilities, gifts, and talents
- It capitalizes on where you are.
- Every person is a leader and already has a God-given group of friends he or she can influence in a positive way.
- *Oikos:* a Greek word translated "house" or "household"—the basic building block of society.

Believe in the Lord Jesus, and you will be saved—you and your household. (Acts 16:31)

Our *oikos* is our personal community—our sphere of influence—people with whom we spend significant time. It is through these relationships that the gospel most frequently spreads. Most people come to Christ with the aid of a family member or friend. The free-market small group system is the perfect environment for drawing unbelievers within your *oikos*, using various interests.

Just remember *why* you are.

MANNA'S "TRIANGLE"

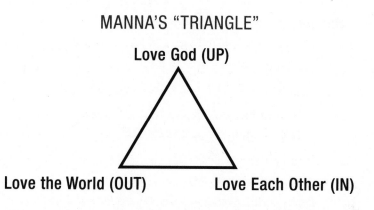

Love God (UP)

Love the World (OUT)   Love Each Other (IN)

- Making disciples doesn't require going to a seminar or taking people through a booklet; it requires being intentional about helping the people around you right now to grow toward Christ.

Making Disciples = Relationships + Intentionality

Everyone is a minister. Everything can be a ministry. People connect most naturally with others who are like them. Common interests, ideas, studies, practices, hardships—these make the best framework for relational connectivity. Good ministry starts where you are, allowing you to capitalize on your natural strengths.

Types of Groups (Time to Dream)

- Interests/passion-based
  What could you start today with no preparation?

- Gift/skill-based
  How has God gifted you and how can you give back?
- Burden-based
  What social or injustice issue keeps you up at night?
- Service-based
  When in doubt, serve one another and the on-looking world!
- Ministry/theme-based
  Bible study, marriage, parenting, new believers
- Community/neighborhood-based
  All about relationships from start to finish
- Weekend experiences
  Taking the small group DNA to our SERVE team groups

LET'S DREAM TOGETHER!

- What are the kinds of groups and ministries in which your heart is inclined to engage?
- If you were to lead a small group, what would be its theme?

Start working through Manna's *Small Group Guide to Getting Started*.

WEEK 6: SMALL GROUPS IN ACTION

M^3: Three goals of small groups (meet, mentor, multiply)

Meet: *Fellowship (Quality Time with Other Christians)*

- Your small group should be a place where individuals meet, connect with one another, build relationships, and have the opportunity to form friendships. It's where people do life together, not just another event to attend.
- Friendship = quality time + shared interests
- We were created by a relational God to have relational needs for significant connection.
- We are created to be at our best when we are in Christ-centered, life-giving relationships (Acts 2:42–47).
  - The Word
  - Fellowship
  - Taking care of needs
  - Prayer/worship
  - Outreach
- Create an environment that welcomes both churched and unchurched.
- Small groups are the most effective way of closing the back door of our church. We never worry about losing people who are connected to a small group.
- People stick because of relationships.
- If at all possible, have fun! Eat good food! Enjoy fellowship!

Mentor: *Helping Grow Balanced, Effective Disciples (More About This in Week 7)*

Discipleship = Relationships + Intentionality

- Small groups are the best environments for believers to influence one another toward becoming more like Jesus and walk in their God-given purposes.
- Your small group should be a place that allows believers to discover, develop, and deploy their spiritual and natural gifts.
- Your role as a mentor is to help each small group participant progress in their journey with Jesus and their next levels of faith.
- If you are a small group leader, come alongside your folks, get to know them, believe in them, encourage them, pray for them. (You are not alone as a leader. Manna-site leaders are there for you to coach you in your leadership journey.)

Multiply

- MULTIPLY DISCIPLES: outreach is the heartbeat of "church" (remember Manna's DNA, our culture) and should be an ongoing aspect of small groups. Manna small groups are passionate and consistent about reaching the lost.
- OUTREACH MIND-SET: your small group can serve as a venue to spur on your participants to see and do their part in helping the lost around them come to know Jesus.
  - PRAY: take the lead in praying for the unchurched.

- **INVITE:** every person can invite an unchurched friend from their *oikos*.
- **WELCOME:** be ready for them to show up!
- **GO:** take at least one step outside your comfort zone as a group to reach out.
- Your small group should engage in at least one community outreach activity.
  - As a group: prayer walks, hospital visits, food giveaways, donations, servant-evangelism, and the like
  - Getting behind some of your site's outreach initiatives

DEVELOPING A MULTIPLICATION MIND-SET

- LeaderStep *can't* be the only place leadership development happens at Manna.
- We want to not only multiply *disciples*, we want to multiply *leaders* (empower and release leaders) and to multiply *groups* (reproduce). Multiplication is more than an activity; it's a mind-set.
- Be intentional about identifying leaders. Look for G.I.F.T.S.
  G *Gifted:* look for people with strengths and talents in leadership (communicating, organizing, motivating, relating, strategizing).

I *Influential:* look for people who already have influence. When they speak, people listen; when they move, people watch and follow.

F *Fruitful:* look for people who get the job done. When they set their hand to work, they produce results.

T *Trustworthy:* look for people who have strong ethics and character. They do what they say they will do. Integrity cannot be taught overnight.

S *Servant:* look for people who are already serving, even though they might not be a "leader." They don't wait to be told; they initiate acts of service.

- Learn to "shoulder tap"
- Look for I.D.E.A.S.

I *Instruction:* verbally teach them practical principles to help them understand what you want them to do.

D *Demonstrate:* model what those truths should look like in real life.

E *Experience:* give them first-hand experience; let them give it a shot.

A *Assessment:* provide helpful evaluation afterward and help them interpret it.

S *Shoulder tap:* "You know, you'd be good at—" Identify other people with leadership potential.

People do what people see. Live loud for Jesus and bring others with you!

JUST A REMINDER: to be a small group leader (or coleader) at Manna, one must have NextStep, completed Manna's membership process, and LeaderStep.

WEEK 7: UNDERSTANDING MENTORING

"Mentoring is a relational experience
in which one person empowers another
by sharing God-given resources."
—P. Stanley and J. R. Clinton, *Connecting: the Mentoring
Relationships You Need to Succeed in Life*, 1992, p. 38

Growing in your ability to effectively mentor people (individuals or groups) is crucial to growing as a leader.

Effectively *managing expectations* is crucial to effective mentoring and leadership.

Models of Mentoring

INTENSIVE MENTORING

Intensive mentoring calls for much more deliberate and specific actions by both the mentor and mentee.

The Discipler

This is a relational process whereby the person who is more experienced in the things of God and the basics of the

Christian life teaches, models, and trains the person who is less experienced.

Four basic areas of concern:

DEVOTIONS: regular times of meeting with God
WORD INTAKE: how to read, memorize, meditate upon, and study Scripture
RELATIONSHIPS: the importance of fellowship and community
MINISTRY: spiritual gifts, evangelism, prayer, serving others

- Help them develop strong, sound, biblical habits.
- As with all intensive mentoring relationships, males mentor males, and females mentor females.
- Evaluate your own devotional life, Word intake, relationships, roles, and participation in ministry.

The Spiritual Guide

This is a relational process in which a person facilitates the spiritual development of others at critical times in their life journeys. The spiritual guide helps shape internal motivations, develops new understanding, and promotes one toward a new level of spiritual maturity.

- Focus on accountability in specific growth areas, such as marriage, finances, and moral freedom.

- The aim is to develop the inner person—who is he or she trying to become?
- Being oriented and focused on outcomes, such as becoming a godly husband, content in your finances, or disciplined in lifestyle to achieve moral freedom.
- Deals with inner motivation and drives, perspectives and passions, and convictions and core values.
- This type of mentoring is usually issue or need focused.

The Coach

This is a relational process in which the mentor helps the mentee develop a new set of skills or increase the skill set he or she already possesses.

- The spiritual guide is interested in *becoming* and focused on *outcomes*, and on imparting one life to another. The coach is interested in *doing* and focused on *behaviors*, in helping someone improve in or learn a skill.
- While the spiritual guide deals with inner drives and motivations, the coach deals with skill sets.
  - Spiritual Guide:
    - own a biblical philosophy of handling money
    - become other-centered (not selfish) in marriage
  - Coach:
    - be able to create a budget
    - learn how to communicate with your spouse

- A person needs mentoring from a coach when faced with a task beyond his or her present capacity to handle (key word = *task*). Again, the focus is on *do*, not *be*.

Going Deeper

- With which of the three intensive models do you most identify? Explain.
- At which of the models would you like to become better? Why?
- How would you go about doing that?

OCCASIONAL MENTORING

These models describe mentors who provide input into the lives of others at appropriate times.

The Counselor

This is a person whom God uses to give timely advice, impartial perspective, or specific guidance to another person. This mentoring relationship can be as brief as a divine contact, or as long as a relationship with a trusted person from whom one seeks advice over a lifetime.

- The spiritual guide deals with *being* and the coach with *doing*. The counselor deals with *advice*.

Eight major empowerment functions of a counselor:

- **ENCOURAGEMENT:** affirms the person is on the right track and can succeed on the road ahead. Points out what God appears to be doing in the life of the mentee
- **SOUNDING BOARD:** provides a listening ear and offers feedback when it is requested or needed
- **MAJOR EVALUATION:** points out errors or pitfalls in thinking, process, or behavior
- **PERSPECTIVE:** offers fresh perspective on or insights into the situation at hand. Relates the present micro-situation to the big picture
- **SPECIFIC ADVICE:** provides input into the decision-making process and offers alternative courses of action or thought
- **LINKING:** connects the mentee with the resources necessary to meet the challenges ahead (people, information sources, finances)
- **MAJOR GUIDANCE:** clarifies options, relates the present circumstances to life stages and the bigger picture, and suggests possible courses of action to a mentee at a major turning point in his or her journey
- **INNER HEALING:** helps people overcome internal hindrances to their progress in their life journeys (usually a trained counselor)

The Teacher

This model of mentor is concerned with imparting knowledge, information, and understanding on a particular subject that is necessary to help the mentee along in his or her life journey.

- The spiritual guide deals with *being*, the coach with *doing*, and the counselor with *advice*. The teacher deals with *information*.
- This relationship can range from formal (as in a classroom) to very informal. (Not every classroom teacher is a mentor to everyone in the class just because he or she is teaching the class.)
- As opposed to the coach who focuses on doing ("How do I do this?"), the teacher focuses on imparting the information the mentee needs to take the next step or be more effective in their present life circumstances ("Where can I find out about . . . ?" or "What do you know about . . . ?").

The Sponsor

This person is a connection maker, linking the mentee to people in an organization or network in such a way as to provide opportunities to the mentee that he or she would not otherwise have had.

- The sponsor is a person who is *in* at a level the mentee is not (influence, reputation, organizational knowledge or recognition). The actions of the sponsor are designed to bring the mentee *in*, or at least to open the doors that lead *in*.

- Not every person who is *in* has the heart or desire to bring others in. Nor should it be expected that every person who is *in* act as a sponsor to just anyone. The sponsor's mentoring is a relationship of trust, because the sponsor's reputation is on the line to some extent.

- Every organization needs those who serve as wise sponsors on behalf of the next generation of participants. Not only do they help the individuals they sponsor, but they help the organization develop at a faster rate.

- Sponsors can and should have some type of ongoing, organic relationship with the mentees to guide them as needed in their journeys within the organization or network, such as explaining unwritten rules, acquainting the mentee with past history, guiding the mentee around certain organizational pitfalls, or interpreting policy.

Going Deeper

- With which of the three occasional models do you most identify? Explain.
- At which of the models would you like to become better? Why? How would you go about doing that?

PASSIVE MENTORING

Passive mentors may seem more like models than mentors, because the mentee has very little (if any) personal contact with them. These individuals are legitimate mentors, however, because the lives of the mentees are impacted by the mentors, even at a distance.

The Contemporary Model

This is a person whose work, ministry, writings, reputation, and character have elevated him or her in the eyes of the mentee, to the point where his or her life and work help shape those of the mentee.

- The contemporary model lives out the values that you hold dear.
- The contemporary model may or may not know that he or she is serving as a model to you. Even if they do, they make no attempt at a personal relationship. In this way, the passive model differs from all other mentoring styles. You follow them; they don't lead you.
- Occasionally, a contemporary model may feel prompted to reach out to a person they perceive as holding them in high esteem. When this happens, there is potential for a shift to a different type of mentoring relationship.
- Three key functions of a contemporary model:
  - Embody key values

- Serve as a role model (model parent, leader, spouse, pastor, believer)
- Their lives serve as road maps for how to live out those values.
- The impact of the contemporary model is threefold:
  - The mentee gains confidence in the veracity of their values.
  - The mentee gains hope that they, too, can live out these values.
  - The mentee is motivated by the example of the mentor.

The Historical Model

This is a person from Scripture or history who is deceased, yet continues to inspire the mentee through autobiographical or biographical writings through his or her own written work, or through his or her contribution to the lives of others.

- This model provides the same basic functions as the contemporary model, though deceased.

Going Deeper

- Which people in your life have had the most positive impact in the development of your character, talents, and abilities to influence people? Explain.
- Which historical figures have had significant impact in your life? Explain.

WEEK 8: HEALTHY LEADERSHIP

Healthy Leadership: "The Constellation"
Balance: Each one of us needs to be in mentoring relationships with others.

Four Mentorship Venues
- UPWARD: those who are "over" you, mentoring you in some way
- DOWNWARD: those "under" you (whom you are mentoring)
- INTERNAL: peers inside your organization (circle of regular working contacts) from whom you readily give and receive
- EXTERNAL: peers outside your organization (circle of regular working contacts) from whom you readily give and receive

The person who has people around them (all four quadrants) who can speak into their lives has the highest potential for personal health and effectiveness.

Going Deeper
- Who in your life is in each of these four quadrants? List them. Describe their influence in your life, as well as your influence in their lives.
- How will you go about strengthening your life in any of these four quadrants?

Next Steps

- What ministry, service, or leadership roles am I currently in? In what areas am I strong? In what areas do I see a need to be strengthened?
- How will I go about pursuing my development as a leader?
- What ministry/small group do I want to lead (or, at least, learn how to lead)? What are my next steps?
- Work through *Small Groups—Getting Started* notebook.
- Take some steps of faith! (See SERVE Team Pathways sign-up sheet)

Important Information About Manna's Micro-Sites

If you have plans to relocate, due to the military or a career shift, and would like to create an expression of Manna Church where you are going, consider starting a Manna Church micro-site.

WHAT IS A MICRO-SITE?

A micro-site is a gathering of people who are committed to glorifying God by helping to equip people to change their world. It embraces our three values and keeps our name, logo, and growth track.

WHO CAN LEAD A MICRO-SITE?

A micro-site leader must be a Manna member, who has gone through our growth track, to include MultiStep, and fully embraces our culture. You could feel a call to full-time ministry or just be passionate about creating an "expression of Manna Church" where you live, work, or play.

You must also complete an interview with the multiply pastor at Manna Church.

WHERE CAN A MICRO-SITE BE STARTED?

They can be started anywhere, at any time, by anyone who meets the basic requirements to lead one. (NOTE: We will not open a micro-site within a one-hour radius of a city-site unless it is reaching a market that a city-site is not reaching.)

WHAT IS MY NEXT STEP TO STARTING A MICRO-SITE?

If you have not been through NextStep or LeaderStep, make plans to attend. If you have attended NextStep and LeaderStep, you are invited to go through our micro-site leader training, called *MultiStep*. You can begin the process today by going to: https://capefear.mannachurch.org/growthtrack/multistep and filling out the form.

NOTES

CHAPTER 1: THE LEADERSHIP CRISIS

1. Oliver Cann, "Crisis in Leadership Underscores Global Challenges," *World Economic Forum*, 10 November 2014, https://www.weforum.org/press/2014/11/crisis-in-leadership-underscores-global-challenges.

2. Mike Myatt, "A Crisis of Leadership—What's Next?" *Forbes*, 10 October 2013, https://www.forbes.com/sites/mikemyatt/2013/10/10/a-crisis-of-leadership-whats-next/#77b335a45000.

3. Ken Davidoff, "How the Cardinals Became Baseball's Best Franchise," *New York Post*, 8 October 2014, http://nypost.com/2014/10/08/why-the-cardinals-are-the-best-franchise-in-baseball/.

4. Bernie Miklasz, "Bernie: Cards' 81-Game Record Best Since 1944," *St. Louis Post-Dispatch*, 6 July 2015, http://www.stltoday.com/sports/baseball/professional/bernie-cards--game-record-best-since/article_1fc0cbc4-c6b4-547d-801f-ba3a5b9a2f88.html.

CHAPTER 3: THE TRUMP CARD THAT IS CULTURE

1. Samuel Chand, *Cracking Your Church's Culture Code: Seven Keys to Unleashing Vision and Inspiration* (San Francisco: Jossey-Bass, 2010).

CHAPTER 4: CHICK-FIL-A AND THE END OF VOLUNTEERS AT MANNA CHURCH

1. Ken Blanchard and Mark Miller, *The Secret: What Great Leaders Know and Do* (San Francisco: Garrett-Koehler Publishers, 2014).
2. Mark Miller, "6000 Definitions of Leadership and Counting," *Pulse*, 5 June 2015, https://www.linkedin.com/pulse/6000-definitions-leadership-counting-mark-miller.
3. Blanchard and Miller, *The Secret,* 105ff.
4. Ibid., 199–122.
5. Ibid., 119.

CHAPTER 5: THE FOUNDATION OF A LEADERSHIP DEVELOPMENT CULTURE

1. Stephanie Jackson, "The Secret of Great Leaders—An Interview with Mark Miller," *Leadership Network*, 2 April 2013, http://leadnet.org/the_secret_of_great_leaders_an_interview_with_mark_miller/.

CHAPTER 6: SHOULDER TAPPING AND THE WAY TEAMS ARE BUILT

1. John Maxwell, *21 Irrefutable Laws of Leadership* (Nashville: Thomas Nelson, 2007).
2. Ibid., 1.

ABOUT THE AUTHOR

Michael Fletcher has served Manna Church as senior pastor since 1985. In that time he has guided the church's growth from 350 members in 1985 to 8,000 members in 2017. Coupling sound biblical teaching with relevant, practical application and cutting-edge outreach, Michael and the pastoral staff have worked to create a culture at Manna that is others focused—a culture that lifts the advancement of the kingdom of God far above the concept of the stereotypical me church.

Having a missional mind-set, Michael's heart is not only to see God's people equipped to change their world, both locally and internationally, but also for the planting of churches with the same world-changing vision.

Under Michael's leadership, Manna has planted or part-nered to plant nearly 100 churches to date. Michael and the Manna team seek to inspire God's people into lives of active service and love, both at home and around the world. Manna is deeply involved in global missions, actively supporting the advancement of the kingdom of God in 65 countries.

Michael and his wife, Laura, have been married since 1979 and live in Fayetteville with eight children and nineteen grandchildren, and counting! In their spare time, Michael and Laura enjoy training and competing in endurance sports with more than 27 marathons and 3 Iron Man finishes (Michael), 3 ultra-marathons (Michael), and a 50-and a 75-mile Ultra Marathon finish (Laura) to their credit.

ALSO AVAILABLE FROM

LEADERSHIP NETWORK

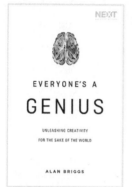

EVERYONE'S A GENIUS
Unleashing Creativity for the Sake of the World

Alan Briggs
9780718042530

TOGETHER
A Guide for Couples Doing Ministry Together

Geoff & Sherry Surratt
9780718095901

THE NEW COPERNICANS
Millennials and the Survival of the Church

David John Seel, Jr.
9780718098872

THE MYTHICAL LEADER
The Seven Myths of Leadership

Ron Edmondson
9780718089191